Song of an Unsung Place
Living Traditions by the Pamlico Sound

by Bill Mansfield
with photographs by Scott Taylor

⊙ Coastal Carolina Press

in collaboration with North Carolina's Northeast Partnership
and the Folklife Program of the North Carolina Arts Council

Song of an Unsung Place: Living Traditions by the Pamlico Sound
by Bill Mansfield

Published by Coastal Carolina Press
in collaboration with North Carolina's Northeast Partnership and the Folklife Program of the North Carolina Arts Council

www.coastalcarolinapress.org

First Edition

Cover photograph by Scott Taylor
Photographs by Scott Taylor and William Mansfield
Historical photographs courtesy of Maxine Simmons
Book design by Whitline Ink Incorporated

Portions of the present work (including selected photographs) appeared in a slightly different version in *The North Carolina Folklore Journal*, Vol. 45, #1, Winter/Spring, (1998). Copyright ©1998 Folklife Program of the North Carolina Arts Council.

Library of Congress Cataloging-in-Publication Data

Mansfield, William, 1953–
    Song of an unsung place : living traditions by the Pamlico Sound / by William Mansfield ; with photographs by Scott Taylor.–– 1st ed.
      p. cm.
    ISBN 1-928556-27-2
    1. Country life—North Carolina—Hyde County. 2. Hyde County (N.C.)—Social life and customs. 3. Hyde County (N.C.)—Description and travel. 4. Country life—North Carolina—Pamlico Sound. 5. Pamlico Sound (N.C.)—Social life and customs. 6. Pamlico Sound (N.C.)—Description and travel.
    I. Taylor, Scott, 1956–   .
    II. North Carolina Arts Council. Folklife Program.
    III. Title.
    F262.H9 M36 2001
    975.6′184—dc21   2001028532

Printed in the USA

Dedicated to the people of Hyde County, whose kindness and generosity made this book possible; and to my wife, whose love and constant encouragement make all things possible.

Table of Contents

Preface

This book began when the Folklife Office of the North Carolina Arts Council asked me to document the folklore and folklife of Hyde County. The term *folklore* embraces a culture's "verbal literature"—jokes, stories, songs, myths, and legends. *Folklife* encompasses the totality of a people's traditions—their occupations, material culture and food, as well as their oral traditions.

The best-known part of Hyde County is Ocracoke; but this picturesque island has attracted many visitors and researchers, so I dedicated my study to the folk culture of the less-celebrated mainland. Because cultural regions are rarely delineated by county lines, my research carried me into the adjoining counties of Beaufort and Tyrell, which share similar geography and heritage.

Between March 1997 and February 1998, I spent several weeks talking with many people from this region. They confirmed Hyde County's reputation for hospitality as they patiently answered my questions about life in their part of North Carolina, and helped me arrive at a better understanding of the place they call home.

Many people helped with this book. I owe thanks to all the folks interviewed, but also to the ones who took the time to offer hospitality and guidance. I especially thank Gene Ballence, Leon Ballence, Buddy Brickhouse, Earl Carawan, Roy Clarke, Annette Gibbs, Mac Gibbs, Grey and Monna Lou Hopkins, Harry Liverman, Martell Marshall, Simon and Becky Martin, Keith and Rosa Mae Mullet, R.S. Spencer, Don Temple, and Ruth Wilson. Paula Bass supplied unlimited enthusiasm and championed this work, as did Feather Phillips of Pocosin Arts. Beverly Patterson and Wayne Martin from the North Carolina Arts Council made this research possible. The Partnership for the Sounds provided invaluable support. Jill Hemming offered encouragement and inestimable advice. Lastly, I thank my wife, Lu Ann Jones, for her love of words and ceaseless support.

Hyde County presents stark vistas: An abandoned building in a newly planted field awaits its end.

Introduction

The mainland of Hyde County presents a stark vista: mile after mile of flat vacant land interrupted by pine forests, expansive fields, drainage ditches, impenetrable swamps and clusters of buildings that may or may not be a town. To many people it looks like the perfect picture of the middle-of-nowhere. Strangers passing through this place usually ask themselves: "How does anyone live here?"

Of course people do live here, and if you talk with them you can get beyond the lonely impressions created by the austere countryside. You discover they like Hyde County's minimalist landscape where "progress" does not obscure the wonder of nature, and where the seasons—rather than a time clock—determine the pace of life.

Mary Helen Cox is someone who prefers wide-open spaces and close contact with nature. She makes crab pots in the workshop behind her house. "It's just pretty here," she'll tell you, her voice keen with enthusiasm. "The land is so rich you can just look at the crops and see them grow."

Marco Gibbs is another native who favors this place. He enjoys the quiet complexity of nature and welcomes the challenge of wrestling his living from the wilderness. He sets traps for the fur-bearing animals that roam the forests and swamps. He uses crab pots made by Mary Helen Cox to catch crabs in the rivers and sounds close to his home.

Listening to their stories adds meaning, and gives significance to, a land that—at first glance—seems a meaningless place.

When Thelma Mooney tells about quilting parties, you understand how people overcame loneliness in this remote place. When Arthur Bryant talks of furnishing music for house parties, he brings to life a close-knit community that provided an appreciative audience for his talents.

Take the time to visit with the people and they will tell you about life here, what makes this place home. They give the land a personality.

Hyde County is one of the first parts of the state that Europeans settled. In the late seventeenth century English colonists arrived in search of fertile, unclaimed land. They found the Native American population (the Secotan Clan of the Algonquin Nation) enjoying the generosity of nature, growing crops and hunting and fishing. The settlers ignored the Indians' claim to the land and pushed them out of the area. By the middle of the eighteenth century the Indians were gone, removed through disease, exile, or assimilation. Although they have disappeared, their strategy for living from the land endures. Then, as now, a large part of the region's economy is based on farming, fishing, and hunting.

While the land proved productive, it also proved protective. The shallow waters of the sounds and the impassible swamps and forests have insulated Hyde County. Since the earliest days of European settlement, no significant in-migration has altered the region's culture. The presence of black people—brought here to work the Europeans' farms—contributes a subtle, yet profound African influence. However, most of the residents, be they black or white, speak with a "down-east" brogue, revealing the dominance of English heritage.

Despite this seeming "timelessness," Hyde County has felt the effect of change. The end of the Civil War saw the region's plantation economy transformed into one of many smaller farms. From 1880 until the early 1920s, lumber companies moved into the area and exploited the forest resources. They brought jobs and prosperity for a while, but took them away when the lumber was depleted.

Long stretches of deserted roads, empty houses and vacant buildings suggest a declining population, and census figures bear this out. The 1900 Census counted 9,278 people living in Hyde County, but population has been in decline ever since. By 1990, it had fallen to 5,411. No industries have moved into the area, and as corporate farming replaces family farms, machines and agricultural chemicals replace the people who once tended the land. They leave to find work and live in more prosperous places.

Yet people remain. How does living here shape their culture? In part, this study answers that question. It also brings the amorphous concept of cultural traditions into sharper focus.

Sometimes it's risky to admit what you learned, because in so doing you reveal what you didn't know. When studying folklore in the classroom, I tended to think about cultural traditions in terms of "items of folklore." That is, I considered individual objects and events—quilts, log cabins, ballads, fiddlers' contests, and square dances—as things isolated from the cultures that spawned them. Conducting research for this project (talking to *different* people from the *same* culture), reminded me that the "items of folklore" are best understood in conjunction with the culture that produces them. The "items of folklore" are like the vines that sprout from a larger subterranean root system—perceptible manifestations of a sprawling but invisible body of thought. As the underground root system and vines that grow from it are shaped by the time and place (context) of their existence, so too is this collective body of thought (folklore) shaped by its time and place.

Like many others, I habitually think of folklore in terms of the past. This research reminded me that folklore is an active part of everyday existence. The content and context of traditions may change, but traditions endure.

Interests in traditional music and occupational folklore guided my research and are central to this work. Unfortunately here, like everywhere else, the influence of popular culture and the power of mass media have overwhelmed musical traditions. While only a scant few can still sing old ballads or know how to call a square dance, many still wrestle a living from the land in the tradition of their ancestors. Not everybody sings, but everybody works.

Elements of folklore are found in all occupations. Novices learn many jobs informally through observation and imitation. All work has "tricks of the trade" and shortcuts that are passed along from one worker to another.

Occupations generate their own language and material culture. Like the stories and jokes that grow out of work, all of these expressions present the distinctive flavor of that job. Exploring the folklore of work best reflects the unique geography, history, and culture of this region.

The three sections of this book—*Traditional Skills*, *Social Life*, and *Belief and Change*—explore different aspects of the area's culture.

In the *Traditional Skills* section, "Working the Land" investigates practices associated with hunting, trapping, and preparing game for the dinner table. The region's unique environment—the swamps, the fields, forests, and sparse population—make it an excellent place for wildlife. In fact, Hyde County is the site of two wildlife reserves, administered by the U.S. Fish and Wildlife Service. Between 1938 and 1972, the hunting lodge at Lake Mattamuskeet welcomed hunters from across the nation and around the world. The occupational folklore connected with wildlife figures prominently in the region's heritage and sense of identity.

"Working on the Water" explores maritime traditions. The region's proximity to the sounds makes working on the water a major career. I investigated the traditions of crabbers, and the skills that support the watermen. I also talked with some boat builders and crab pot makers, and explored the changing customs of making fishing nets.

The *Social Life* section deals with the traditions of quilt-making and music. "Making Music" looks at the local music of eastern Beaufort, Hyde and Tyrrell counties. I explored the traditions of secular and sacred community-based music of both whites and blacks. The separations between secular and sacred, as well as between whites and blacks, are both real and artificial. Many of the people I talked to play only sacred music and consider any other music too worldly. Yet, some talented musicians perform both types of music with equal skill and sincerity. For most of the twentieth century, racial segregation has been a part of the South's laws and customs. Despite this division, members of both races "crossed the color line" for the love of music. Gerald Lee Bryant, a black man, learned guitar from his white neighbor, John Carawan. H. Ray Modlin, a white man, learned guitar from "Slim" Davis, a black farm worker. African-American Arthur Bryant taught the intricacies of blues harmonica *to* white neighbors while learning the banjo *from* whites. These accounts speak of the power of music to transcend racism.

"Quilting Traditions" might seem out of place, but there is enough cold weather to encourage a strong quilting tradition. The women I spoke with made it clear that quilting is more than just sewing—it is an important part of their social fabric.

The *Belief and Change* section is divided into two areas of interest. "Conflict and Change" deals with attitudes towards government, corporate farming, and visiting hunters. "Witch Hunts" explores stories and beliefs about supernatural events.

Though this work presents only a partial picture of the region, it sheds some light on a beautiful part of North Carolina unknown to most outsiders. This book might remind the natives what a good place they call home, and might teach visitors to appreciate tidewater as the natives do.

To many people, mainland Hyde County looks like the perfect picture of "the middle of no where."
Road signs provide directions outside of Engelhard, NC.

Working the Land

You don't see a lot of people out here. Geographic and economic barriers separate the sparse population from the influences of mainstream society. The region's depressed economy contributes to this cultural seclusion; poverty isolates people as effectively as any natural barrier. The isolation challenges the natives and forces them to rely upon their own resources. One of the major resources available to the region is the abundant wildlife. The same factors that restrict human habitation encourage the animal population. An isolated, self-reliant population and a rich wildlife environment create a culture with a strong hunting tradition.

Stories describe the connection between these people and the traditions of hunting. Individuals telling similar stories about separate events indicates the common experience of the region's folk culture. The stories combine to present the character of the region's culture the same way individual threads combine to weave a tapestry. From the time of settlement until the present, natives of this region learned to "live off the land" from their ancestors and through their own experiences.

Extracting a living from the wilderness puts hunters and trappers in conflict with nature. Guarding their personal welfare against state and federal wildlife agencies who seek to regulate hunting can also result in conflicts with authority. Successfully negotiating these conflicts promotes a sense of self-sufficiency and independence.

Joseph Leslie Simmons III poses with a bear slain by his father near Herron Bay, Hyde County, circa 1940.

Folklore of Hunting and Trapping

Hunting and trapping create folklore—concepts and systems of belief that people develop in an attempt to come to terms with tensions generated by dichotomies. Hunting and trapping present several: humanity and nature, insider and outsider, and natural and supernatural.

The humanity/nature opposition should come as no surprise. People who live close to nature and depend upon it will attempt to exert control over this incomprehensible force. William Cutrell tells a story that underscores the economic importance of wildlife, while also illustrating human folly.

They used to trap bear back years ago. You could take a bear and dress him out, and ship him [to Norfolk]. Every Thursday they had a steamboat come up here and pick up eggs and chickens, and stuff that people wanted to ship to Norfolk. He'd bring $75 to $100. That was money along then—big money! And that's the way people made their living.

This old fellow down the road here, Gus Brickhouse, he said, 'If you ever catch [a bear] I want to kill him with a club.' Well, my uncle caught one close to Killkenny Landing. He come out and said, 'Gus, all right now, I got him.'

Gus said, 'How big is he?'

'About 250 pounds.'

'I'm gonna kill him with a club.'

So he went to the woodpile and got him a club, just like he wanted. [My uncle] told him, 'You can't kill that bear with that club.'

'Huh! I'll show you!'

Gus went in there and walked up pretty close to the bear. Then he hauled back and hit him over the head with that club. The bear fell right [over].

'I told you I could kill him with my arm!'

My uncle said, 'You just wait a few minutes.'

Well, that old bear begin to move. Gus walked over to hit him again.

My uncle said, 'No you ain't gonna hit him with him laying down. Now you wait till he gets on his feet.' Well, the old bear got straight and up on his feet.

My uncle said, 'All right, go ahead and kill him.'

Now, old man Gus wore a pair of bib overhauls like these I got on. When he hauled back to hit at the bear, that bear caught the pole with his paw, [and] snatched her right in two. That other foot caught in his overhauls and cut the whole bib of them off, like a razor. Buddy, that man turned white all over, as white as any bleaching you've ever seen.

My uncle told Gus what the bear'd do to him. That bear was watching, and if you ever hit him on the head one time you ain't gonna hit him no more. That's just like trapping him. You set a trap for him, you catch him and he gets out, you won't catch him no more—that's the end of that. He can smell that trap just as good as you can see it. He'll never get caught in it no more.[1]

Gus Brickhouse tried to dominate nature with brute strength, but trappers use a different strategy to bridge the gap between humanity and nature. To be successful they must be able to read the landscape for signs of animal activity. Understanding the evidence left by their prey is not enough. They attempt to think like an animal and, through that process, triumph over the animal.

James Sykes' description of his father's trapping accentuates the trapper's efforts to enter the mind of an animal.

BILL MANSFIELD

"They [wild animals] are much harder to catch than people realize…If a trap ever pinches an animal and he escapes, he'll remember how the trap works." —Marco Gibbs

Mostly, my father's idea was to outwit the animal. He might not even set the trap the first two or three times he looked [at a site]. He might turn around and study what the animal was doing—study the animal's behavior.

1 Some of the interview excerpts presented in this report are edited to make the narratives more concise and coherent.

Once he learned about the animal's behavior, he might just track it. He might look down at its track and see where it's been going, or see if it's been eating in the field.

If an animal was going back and forth between fields, my father would put something there that the animal would have to step across. But he wouldn't set a trap there that first night. He would observe it to see if the animal went across it first. [Dad] would know that the animal was going to cross that log. If the animal would go across it, the next thing that animal knowed, he was caught by the leg.

If it was a log [that served as a bridge across a ditch] he would put it up on the end of the log—most of the time they'll crawl up on the end of it. If it was a log they had to cross, he would put a trap right up next to it on either side. He might use two traps for that one particular place, because that is where the animal will stop, listen and rest.

He would try to out-think the animal, or out-scheme it. He tried to make the animal do what he wanted it to do. And that's what he used to teach us. He was cunning when it come down to trapping.

COURTESY MAXINE SIMMONS

Hyde County's well regarded hunting guide Joe Simmons proudly poses with the results of a successful hunting expedition, circa 1940.

Professional trapper Marco Gibbs provides some theory to support Sykes' practices. When setting a trap he "tries to see a trap the way an animal would." Traps are not set just anywhere he sees evidence of animal activity. Rather, Gibbs sets traps in what he calls "transitional areas"—places where the landscape changes. Candidates for one of the traps include areas where the forest stops and a field begins, where the edges of fields meet, where solid earth gives way to swamp, or where one road intersects another. Perhaps the passage from one type of terrain to another distracts the animal, improving the trap's camouflage. The shifts in landscape might make the animal more open to the idea of change, arousing his curiosity and luring him into the disruption caused by the trap.

Gibbs' serious respect for the animal's "natural" intelligence challenges him to think like animals in order to outwit them.

> They are much harder to catch than people realize. They don't know how much these animals can outsmart you. Especially if one gets "trap-wise." If a trap ever pinches an animal and he escapes, he'll remember how the trap works. He'll be much harder to catch.

In one of his favorite trapping stories, he describes a "trap-wise" raccoon. He observed tracks showing where the animal had crossed two fallen trees. Gibbs set a trap, but the next day found the trap lying upside down and thrown out of its site. Two more traps were set. The following day he found both of them thrown and upside down. On the third attempt, he set the first trap right-side up and the second trap upside down. The trap-wise raccoon threw the first trap, but in throwing the inverted trap he got caught.

Marco Gibbs enjoys trapping. When asked what he likes about trapping he will tell you he enjoys being out-of-doors and close to nature. "Ultimately it's outsmarting the animal," he says. He relishes the opportunity to test his wits against the power of nature, participating in a struggle reaching back to prehistoric times. The stories from Marco Gibbs and James Sykes represent the rich lore generated from the tension between humanity and nature.

Folklife Of Hunting and Trapping

Hunting and trapping generate folklife—such as the practical techniques used to catch and dress animals, and the methods used to cook them.

Some people depend upon hunting and trapping to supplement their diet, while others use wildlife to add to their income. They capture game for sale and also sell their services to visiting hunters who are attracted by the region's reputation for game. Services offered to visiting hunters include acting as guides, providing room and board, and cleaning of game.

While hunting and trapping do not involve as many of the area's residents as they once did, these occupations still play a large role in the region's sense of identity. Even if the inhabitants never hunted or trapped, they are related to, know, or have done business with someone who has. People raised during the Great Depression describe how it put food on the table when jobs and money were scarce, while those born after the Depression talk about the importance of these activities in the lives of their parents—and consider it an important part of their heritage. This association connects them with the larger hunting and trapping tradition.

The important position that hunting and trapping played in generating food and income can be heard in the stories from area residents. James Sykes of Alligator in Tyrrell County speaks for many when he says, "Then, people would hunt any way they could. You'd either hunt or not have enough food to feed the family." Hyde County's Thelma Mooney recalls that trapping provided "what we lived off of in the winter to send the kids to school." Her husband also guided hunters, and Mooney herself earned money by boarding hunters and cleaning their geese. Troy Mayo from Rose Bay recalls guiding hunters in the 1930s "for peanuts, but you made a living at it. You could feed your family and that's what you were interested in. It was hard to feed a family then." About the same time, Seth Bridgeman Credle captured bullfrogs for a biological supply house in the town of Elon College. Carolina Biological Supply paid forty to sixty cents apiece for them. According to Credle, "That was money then."

Glynn Jarvis worked intensely with hunting and trapping. In the late 1930s and throughout the 1940s, his father bought animal hides from trappers in the region.

That was a big business. A raccoon hide at this same time would bring in the unheard of price of $7.50 or $8. Labor on the farm at that time was $15 to $20 a week. He would make more money trapping. Well, he would do both. Everybody trapped back then—even the type of people that had a little country store. All the children [trapped]; that was the first thing they started.

Exposure to this tradition at home taught Jarvis how to trap, stretch hides, and market wild game. He caught bullfrogs and sold them to a local restaurant. When the government rationed meat during World War II, he trapped and sold animals to members of his community. "You could sell every raccoon you'd catch. Some would buy muskrat, but raccoon was the biggest seller." He and his brother peddled the game from their Radio Flyer wagon. "A large 'coon would go for $5 easily. Hamburger was $3.50 a pound but you couldn't get it because of the war."

While hunting and trapping generated food and income, they also inspired a great deal of folklore. Chief among the traditional skills needed for success at either venture is a keen understanding of the landscape and the behavior of the animals that live there. One must be able to read the landscape for signs of animal activity and understand the animals in order to interpret the signs. Hunters and trappers of this area acquired these skills in the most traditional way—from their own experience and from the experience of recognized masters.

Members of the Edward "Bunk" Carawan family are renowned hunters. Here is how he learned to track wildlife: "I hunted a lot when I was a boy," he explained. "I enjoyed hunting. [My father] used to take out deer hunters and I helped him. You'd go in certain areas where you knew deer was running. There you'd put a man. My father worked it, and he knew about the best place to put men out. I went with him." Learning from his father and from his own experiences, Carawan began to understand the ways of animals.

The late Joe Simmons—a prominent Hyde County hunting guide—was born and raised in the eastern Beaufort County community of Haslin. He learned much about tracking and hunting animals from his African-American neighbor, Jack Sykes. Simmons then passed this knowledge on to his wife, children and grandchildren. His widow, Maxine Simmons, explains that Jack Sykes taught her husband to read animal signs, and turned Joe into "an avid tracker; he enjoyed watching for nature." She picked up tricks of the trade by riding with him for over fifty years.

> I learned to do it, too. I learned how to watch [for animals]. He showed me how to look through the trees. I can't tell you how to do it, but you can look through the trees...You can focus your eyes just right. I saw my first deer...and when I saw it, I just like to had a fit. To me that was a big accomplishment, to be able to look through the trees and see that whole deer. It just opened up the woods for me.

Joe Simmons' daughter Betty Mann adds, "We used to [joke] about sending children to him for 'Daniel Boone training.'"

Learning to read the ground, trees, and bushes for signs of animal activity is one aspect of the hunting and trapping tradition. Learning to make and set the traps is another. James Sykes learned the art of setting traps from his father, who was "a great hunter and a good trapper."

> He made little snares. Taught us how to make snares. To make a snare you'd bend a tree limb over and put a small rope in there—'bout enough to hold the game. When the rabbit goes through there he'll trip the snare, and it will catch him right by the neck and hang him—hang him right there!
>
> Same thing with possums and foxes, anything else he decided to catch. Every time he caught something he didn't need a steel trap. You can make a trap out of a rope or a piece of small cable.
>
> There was a fence line there, and you could see real well where an animal had been going back and forth through the fence. He taught us how to look real close and tell what kind of animal it was by the hair it left on the fence. He was sharp about that kind of stuff.

Snares were just one type of homemade "folk trap." William Cuthrell made a "live trap" to catch robins and other small songbirds. He began by arranging sticks horizontally to form a pyramid-like "cage." Bait placed in the base of the pyramid lured birds into the trap. Space between the sticks allowed them in, but the sticks prevented them from hopping out. This trap allowed the birds to be taken alive.

Cuthrell preferred a "dead fall" trap for taking small birds. The dead fall trap is made from a board with one end placed on the ground, and the other end propped up with a stick. Cuthrell calls the stick a "treadle." Birds are lured under the board when bait is spread beneath it. When they pull at the bait—which is attached to the treadle—the stick is dislodged and the board falls on the birds and kills them.

Maxine Simmons used a variation of this trap for robins. She attached a string to the stick that supports the board, and at the proper moment pulled the string. The board fell and "kill[ed] the birds without messing them up."

While growing up during the Depression, Rose Bay native Troy Mayo caught ducks with baited hooks. He explained the economic necessity and improvisational nature of trapping:

> There was five boys and three girls in our family, and we done what you had to do to eat. Gun shells were hard to come by. You'd take a line and tie some hooks and weights on it, and put a grain of corn on the hook. That duck would dive down there and get that grain of corn and the weight would hold him down. There was always a way to get game if you didn't have a gun shell.

When James Sykes was young, he used steel traps to capture ducks.

> You'd see them in the pond and say, 'Let's catch us a duck.' We'd get one of Daddy's steel traps,

wade out there, and throw a little corn out. The next thing you'd know, he'd be flapping and flapping, and we'd go out there and hit him in the head. We'd pick him and prepare him for eating.

Perhaps the most unique improvisation for trapping is George Bush's use of crab pots to catch fur-bearing animals. His story reinforces the traditional aspect of trapping. It was his friend and neighbor Warren Ross who introduced him to trapping, but an African-American trapper in New Holland suggested the unlikely phenomenon of trapping with a crab pot.

> I trapped all the ditches. I was catching minks and raccoons. A black man down the canal bank in New Holland told me I could catch 'coons in a crab pot. I didn't know if you could or not, but I had some extra [crab pots]. I thought, 'I'll see.' I took these crab pots and caught 'coons in them.
>
> I caught five 'coons in a crab pot in one day. Had to shoot them in the head with a .22 rifle to get 'em out of there. Went on to the rest of my traps, and I had caught a couple of minks and 'coon and muskrats. [Returned to the crab pot and] I could see something moving. Bless God! That crab pot had caught two more 'coons!

A mass-produced, factory-made steel trap cannot be considered a traditional object, but the knowledge a trapper uses to set the trap can be entirely traditional. The trapper learns to set the trap in such a way that it is imperceptible to the prey. This information is generally passed along from the experienced trapper to the novice.

James Sykes explains in detail how his father set a trap so that it was unnoticed by the keen sight and sense of smell of the animal.

> When I was a boy, I caught myself mocking [imitating] my dad. Most of the time we would put them [traps] in the chicken house overnight—throw them in there and the chickens would roost over them [eliminating the human scent].
>
> We tried not to handle the trap any more than necessary. If we handled them, we tried to get an old tow sack and handle it with that to keep our scent off it. They'd want that chicken scent, but they don't want your scent.
>
> If Mama would kill chickens, we'd save the chicken intestines and smear it on [the trap]—the chicken fat and stuff—to keep them from smelling you after you've set it.
>
> You want [the trap set] in the path. You want to clean out a little spot and set it, and put light twigs over it—twigs and light grasses. You want to handle it with sticks or something. You don't want to take your hand and do it; you want to do it with a stick. He will smell that chicken fat and

Marco Gibbs began trapping as a young boy. He is currently one of the most skillful and successful in Hyde County.

start nosing around, and the next thing you know, you have him by the front foot.

James Sykes' discussion of setting traps—a term used to describe "arming" the trap to be sprung, and positioning the trap to capture an animal—suggests the skill involved in trapping.

Observing expert Hyde County trapper Marco Gibbs provides an example of the current methods for setting traps. Gibbs is a recognized expert on wildlife of the region. However, his knowledge about trapping was not easily won.

> My immediate family were mostly into hunting…but there was quite a few other people around here that [trapped]. At these old country stores I'd hear people talk about trapping, especially trapping bears. That really caught my attention.

When he turned to these veteran trappers for advice and guidance, he discovered not all were willing to help—in fact some attempted to discourage competition by misleading him.

> [Some] people were real secretive about trapping. None of these people would tell you anything. In fact, they would give me misinformation, suggesting something crazy. I remember trying two or three of them, and after a couple of times I figured [the deception] out.

Gibbs eventually found a mentor who helped him perfect his trapping skills. He went on to become one of the region's most successful trappers.

During eastern North Carolina's trapping season (December 15–February 28), Gibbs covers an area that includes parts of Beaufort, Dare, Hyde, and Tyrrell counties. As soon as one season ends, he begins to prepare for the next. Readying his traps a year in advance allows ample time for the scent of humans to fade. He cleans, adjusts, and dyes each trap. He explains that dyeing them "keeps them from rusting, hides the scent, and helps them blend in."

If Gibbs is particular in preparing a trap, he is especially careful about where the trap is set. He places the trap in an area where animals are likely to encounter it. Years of experience have taught him to read the landscape and detect signs of the presence of animals. These signs include footprints, trails worn into the terrain, droppings, and clues that an animal has been feeding in the area.

> Every time I go somewhere I'm looking, scouting for places to run trap lines…I look for trails, logs, bridges, creeks, canals, and places where animals cross the highway. Good food in a good

location makes a good trap site. Wind direction is important, too. In this area the wind blows from the north in the wintertime. You set your traps on the north side of where the animals are traveling. The wind will blow the scent of the bait to the animal and lure them to the trap.

When he goes out to set a trap he takes along everything required to camouflage it. His equipment includes a pail of loose dirt, a collection of gall bush branches, and a tool kit. Inside the tool kit he keeps a house painter's brush, a sieve, a one-foot square foam rubber pad, a masonry hammer, a small set of shrubbery clippers, a pair of rubber gloves, several dowels, several three-inch squares of fine meshed screen wire, a couple of tightly sealed jars of pungent lures, and a spray bottle containing fox urine. As he uses this equipment to set the trap, Gibbs displays all the concentration of an artist at work.

His techniques vary with the type of trap he adopts. One option is the "Conibear trap." Named after its inventor, this trap stands vertically and closes on the animal as it passes through. The more conventional (and better known) leg-hold trap sits horizontally on the ground and closes on the animal's leg when it steps in.

Gibbs places the Conibear trap in an area with fairly thick undergrowth in a path that the prey is likely to use. Because this trap stands erect, its installation is less disruptive to the landscape than horizontal traps. He uses branches of nearby bushes for camouflage, twining them around the trap's frame. They are also arranged to encourage the animal to pass through the trap by suggesting the best route. Sometimes fallen branches or other naturally occurring obstacles are positioned to guide the animal into the trap.

The leg-hold trap is another option. This trap rests on the ground and requires a different type of painstaking effort to camouflage. To begin, Gibbs scoops a shallow hole out of the earth to conceal the trap. Next, he uses a masonry hammer to soften the earth and remove the loosened dirt. Gibbs positions the trap in the depression and places a small square of screen wire over the trap's pan, or "trigger." Using a dowel, its edges are carefully tucked under the trap's jaws to prevent the dirt from fouling the trigger mechanism.

Next, he covers the trap with a thin layer of dirt, giving it a more natural look by sifting it through a sieve. A tool called the trapper's cap is placed over the pan, and a heavier layer of dirt is then sifted over the trap. The trapper's cap creates a slight depression that both marks the pan's location and resembles a paw print, attracting a curious animal. Once the trap is concealed, he uses a paintbrush to evenly distribute a final covering of dirt. For further camouflage, he removes the trapper's cap and sifts a handful of dried grass and leaves through the sieve.

The last step of the leg-hold trap's installation is situating the lure and bait. With an aroma that resembles a decomposing animal, the lure's strong smell draws the prey to the trap site. Gibbs often takes advantage of the prevailing wind direction when positioning the lure. Sometimes the lure is a "sight attracter"—an object that will arouse the animal's curiosity. "For some reason," Gibbs reports, "old-fashioned porcelain door knobs attract otters." The bait—which looks and smells like a small animal's innards—is placed close to the trap's pan.

Step 1

Step 2

Step 3

Step 4

BILL MANSFIELD

Trapper Marco Gibbs demonstrates artistic qualities of the trade. Notice how he sculpts the landscape to conceal his work.

While the lure draws the prey *to* the trap site, the bait draws the prey *into* the trap.

Regardless of the type of trap, Gibbs believes a disruption in the landscape makes an animal suspicious. To maintain the environmental integrity of the site, he uses materials from the immediate area to hide the trap. If no materials are available nearby he will use the dirt from his pail and his "imported" gall bush branches. When he sets the trap, he kneels upon a foam rubber pad. The pad not only provides a comfortable place to rest his knees, but also minimizes his impact on the trap site by reducing the appearance of knee prints and hiding his scent.

To eliminate the smell of the traps, Gibbs soaks them in a commercially produced solution and coats the trap with paraffin. He wears rubber gloves when setting his traps. To further conceal the taint of humans, he sprays the trap site with a liberal dose of fox urine, an aromatic substance purchased from fox farms.

The dedication that Marco Gibbs brings to trapping clearly demonstrates the trade's artistic qualities. He carefully reads the countryside for evidence of animal activity, and uses this information to locate the trap site strategically. He presides over each installation, adroitly sculpting the landscape to conceal his work.

Percy Carawan, who learned to make decoys from his father, shows an unfinished decoy outside his workshop in Gull Rock, Hyde County.

Making Decoys

The decoys used to lure waterfowl in range of a hunter's gun are an important part of hunting traditions. In recent years handmade decoys also have become highly collectible items of folk art. One of Hyde County's best-known decoy makers is Percy Carawan. Born in 1910 on Goose Creek Island in Pamlico County, he now lives in Hyde County's Gull Rock community. Percy Carawan has farmed, fished, worked as a carpenter, worked in a shipyard, guided hunters, and trapped. He is passionate about nature, and would rather be in the woods observing wildlife than any place else.

> There was nothing in this world any prettier to me than a bunch of geese coming in [to land] and setting their wings…drop their feet out and hit that water. That was the prettiest sight I'd ever seen.

Making decoys is a tradition in Carawan's family.

> My dad made decoys back there 'fore I was born. He made working decoys. He'd make a sleeping duck with his neck turned right around. Looked like his bill stuck in his down. My dad was a man that could do anything he wanted to do.

Carawan makes decoys like his father. With a hatchet, he roughs out a block of juniper wood to form the decoy's body. He uses a wood rasp—or more recently an electric sander—to complete the shaping. To make the head and neck of the bird, he uses roots from a black gum tree that are naturally curved in a similar way to a bird's neck.

> I go in the woods and go in a black gum swamp. You'll find these roots that come up out of the ground, turn and go back down. Then I get this crook [to make the head and neck]. If you put a head up there sawed from a board, it will split right off. If you hit it, it will split. A gum root won't. My daddy always made them out of gum roots. I make them out of roots.

Carawan keeps wood for decoys floating in a bathtub in the yard close to his workshop. The wet wood is soft and easier to work. "You can cut that like a potato when it's green [wet], but if you let it dry, it's just as hard as flint." Some craftspeople make decoys into accurate, life-like productions of birds, but Carawan prefers simpler decoys—like his father did.

> I just make a working decoy. I don't make a fancy decoy. I'm not good enough to make real fancy decoys. A wooden block—a [homemade] decoy—a wild goose will come to it quicker than he will a boughten decoy. I don't care how pretty they are. [Manufactured decoys] are too light and bob around too much. A wooden decoy…they lay on the water like a goose. When a bunch of geese comes in with them [decoys] just sitting there, nodding in the water, they look like geese. It's because of the way they set on the water and hang to the lines. Real geese do not jerk about on the water. Wooden decoys ride the water like a real goose…The goose knows more than the man—unless the man's got experience.

To make the decoy ride the water realistically Carawan will balance the finished bird. He prefers sheet lead attached to the decoy's bottom with galvanized or copper nails, which won't rust.

Although Carawan does not make "fancy" decoys, he is aware of the collector's market. Currently his decoys sell for several hundred dollars. He remembers a time when decoys were not so valuable. One summer, he and a friend made one hundred decoys. They sold those they did not keep for five dollars each, and used the rest for firewood. Folk art collectors will pay more for "authentic" decoys that look old and used. Some makers fraudulently "age" their decoys to increase their value. One aging technique is to leave the new decoy in a ditch covered with wet leaves for a month or more. Some attempt to create the impression of a working decoy by attaching an old bolt as a weight, or even by shooting it with birdshot.

Because he is deeply rooted in the tradition, Percy Carawan's decoys need no such shortcuts. He does not need to "age" his decoys. He laughs and exclaims, "People want my decoys because of *my* age."

Tanning Hides and Cleaning Birds

Once an animal is trapped, skinning the animal and preparing its hide for sale requires another range of skills. Now that deep freezers are common appliances, most trappers sell fur "in the round"—that is, attached to the animal. But retired trappers still remember how to skin animals and prepare their hides.

Glynn Jarvis learned to dress hides from his father, a fur buyer. Jarvis used this skill to dress hides he and his father bought "in the round" from other trappers.

The trapper had a place out around the barn where he prepared his hides. Had his own curing boards. The boards were made out of beautiful material, it was juniper…cypress. It was light and thin; the boards were a work of art.

We had a building out in the back of our home called the "fur house." Inside we had a skinning room and drying room. We had big beautiful boards to fit any type of fur, from an otter down to a mink. Then we had racks that would store thousands of hides.

It's an art the way you dress [a hide]. I had to learn. When I learned to skin I had to start on a possum, because the possum was the cheapest thing. First you would cut around his feet. After you cut around his feet, you went up about three inches into his belly. You had to pull the whole thing off. You'd have the hole for the mouth, and the ears'd still be intact. Then you'd put it on a board with the skin part out, and the fur would be next to the board. We had a drawing knife that we used to scrape the fat from the hide. Then you'd let that cure. We just air dried it.

We might go and trim it up, and we would comb it and brush it. If we had mink that didn't have a real good color, my father had some real nice dye and a brush. [We used] all the tricks of the trade. It's like the man selling strawberries, always put the big strawberries on top. If it pleases the eye…

Tradition and "tricks of the trade" translated into profits. Buyers graded the furs on feel and texture. As Jarvis explains, "The better it was prepared on the board, the more money it would bring. The trapper took a great pride in preparing his fur." The art of dressing hides for fur buyers figured prominently in the region's economy and tradition.

Dressing waterfowl for visiting sportsmen occupied a smaller economic niche, but is no less important in the area's heritage. Birds were much more convenient for visiting hunters to carry home after they were cleaned and dressed. Those who "picked" the ducks, swans, and geese played an important role in the local economy. Thelma Mooney cleaned birds for her family, friends, and the hunters that her husband guided. Whether she received payment for picking the birds or not, she kept the feathers and put them to use. Her story reveals the skill required to clean a bird efficiently.

What I'd do is take my table and clear it off. Get everything ready and have a bag for the good feathers, and a bag for the bad feathers. You could take the goose and pick it here on the table and take your time and not have feathers all over. But you take somebody to come in and say, 'I can help you pick'—like a man half-drunk—I had feathers all over the house. [Laughs]. I'd pick them [feathers] off. Pick them feathers so you don't strow them. You just pick slowly and deliberately. Put your feathers in the bag.

I had them by the bag. I made one feather bed. And I made pillows—right many pillows. I made a little baby pillow out of nothing but the down off of one. I just picked the big feathers off and made a pillow out of the down. Then I give them [feathers] to sisters, and brothers, and in-laws and let them make their own pillows.

Then cut your wings off. I save the wings to dust with. That's what I always used a swan's wing or a goose's wing [for]. They're [t]he best for dusting your blinds. [Next] I'd take them and put them in that hot boiling water and get the rest of the feathers all off. After I done that, I'd swinge [singe] the rest off on the oil stove that I cooked on. Then I'd take them and gut them. When I fixed one it was all ready to put in and bake, or cut it up and put in the pot.

"Picking birds" was usually left to people pushed to the economic margins. Guides regularly arranged to have their birds cleaned. Betty Mann, daughter of hunting guide Joe Simmons, explains what would usually happen.

BILL MANSFIELD

There was always colored families that would pick the geese. [The hunters] just dumped them all in a pile; carried them down there [to be picked], and then went back and got them.

Today, a home in Hyde County's Goshen community displays a handcrafted sign that boldly announces: WE CLEAN BIRDS. It is

SCOTT TAYLOR

Born in 1919, Dorthy Collins (left) still cleans birds for hunters. She is seen here with her sister, Lillian Spencer, in Hyde County's Goshen community.

the home of Dorothy Collins, an African-American woman who still cleans birds for hunters. Born in 1919, she learned how to clean fowl from her parents. Initially, hunting guides delivered birds for her to clean. As her reputation spread, hunters brought birds to her of their own volition.

All the people I worked for loved my picking. They'd say so and come in and give me tips. There's one [hunting guide] down here now that loves the way I pick the birds. Some of them will pick 'em and won't clean them good when it gets down to them pin feathers. I've sat many times with a towel in my lap and a knife in my hand and pull 'em out, pull 'em out, pull 'em out—until I get them clean.

I fix them like you bought them to the store. Take them, cut them in two places, and then you put the feets up there and that makes [the birds] small, and you puts them in the bag. They likes the way I saved the gizzards and the livers and put them inside. Like what my mama always said: 'What you do, do it right and do it clean.'

A lot of them [other pickers] just clean 'em, gut them, wash them, and put them in a bag— and that's it.

Loyal customers and generous tips were Collins' rewards for her attention to detail.

Tips, that's where you make your money. I make good money when they give you tips. This here man comes down from Virginia and stays to his son's. When he goes back, he cleans out his freezer and brings me [the extra food].

One Sunday there was a lawyer down here—he was a colored guy and his wife. They go and get the ducks in the sound. They'd been out all that Saturday…That Saturday night he come and say, 'My wife cleans birds, but she's gone. I know you picks, so I brought 'em out here.' I look and say, 'How many is it?' He had right many. He say, 'I wants to leave by twelve o'clock tomorrow. Can you handle these by then?' I say, 'Yes sir, I'll try.'

Saturday night, I commence picking on them birds. That Sunday morning when he come pick them up, you know what he lay in my hands? One hundred dollars—that's for cleaning the birds! Then he give me a fifty dollar tip!

Not every hunter employed local people to clean their birds. Martin Armstrong tells an amusing story concerning some men with an unusual method for dressing their geese:

We had some hunters from Santee, South Carolina. There were eight of them, and they were a rough group. At that time, the limit was two geese a day per man. They killed their limit and I asked them what they wanted to do with their geese. We had colored people that would dress geese for fifty or seventy-five cents…

They didn't want their geese cleaned. After about three days I said, 'If you don't clean these geese, damn if they ain't going to rot.' The first one they had killed had done turned green! They just bundled them up when they got ready to leave. That's the way they were going to carry them home.

I said, 'What are you going to do with them damn rotten geese?' They said, 'We're going to eat them. We'll pack them in clay just like they are, then we'll cook them. We'll take them out, tear them open, and pick the meat right off of them.'

I said, 'Damn if it don't kill every damn one of you!' And it must have. I ain't seen one of them since. [Laughs]. I wouldn't eat one of them geese for hell and high water! Damn a-mighty! [Laughs].

Dressing Game

For the sportsmen who hired Dorothy Collins to pick birds, hunting represented a leisure activity and was a mark of their success. For most natives of this region hunting was a necessity, and properly preparing wild game played a crucial part of their diet. Living in a place where wild game is plentiful and a regular addition to the menu, people learned how to cook it from their family and community.

The first step in preparing game comes in dressing the animal—separating the edible parts from the inedible parts. Knowing where and how to cut the carcass is passed from expert hunter to novice. Jack Sykes taught Joe Simmons about hunting and the art of dressing game. Joe Simmons then taught all of his children and grandchildren. Maxine Simmons explains:

> Joe Simmons was very meticulous in dressing his game. He always brought good, well-cleaned meat to the table. You'd get impatient watching them clean venison, they took so much time. But it was cleaned right.

The key to "clean meat" was avoiding the scent glands and preventing contact between hide and flesh. James Sykes' family taught him how to clean game.

> Whenever Mom used to clean she would always take the musk sack from around the neck and under the arm and behind the legs. It's called "musking" it. If you're going to eat it, you're going to have to get that musk all off. Skin it all off, 'cause if you try to cook it, you're going to mess up the whole thing.
>
> I noticed whenever they are skinning a[n animal] they try hard not to let the hide touch the meat. You want to keep the hair off of the flesh that you're planning to eat. That will give a different taste to it.

Learning to remove these parts requires developing a knowledge of *what* to remove, as well as a feel for *how* to remove it.

Something for the Table

Coming from a culture that relies upon game for food, James Sykes understands why it has a unique flavor, and how best to prepare it for the table.

I got some experience from cooking for myself from the time I was twelve years old. If I'd go out and kill a rabbit, Mama'd say, 'Well, it's your rabbit, you clean it. You fix it.' So that's what I would do. I'd skin it and prepare it myself, and she'd say, 'If it tastes good enough for you then somebody else may eat it. If it tastes so bad that you don't want it, then you're going to have to get rid of it.' [Laughs].

Game is not grain fed. It eats grasses and twigs, nuts, berries—anything it can. It's going to have a different taste, a strong taste. You take a hog, you feed it, and it goes and lays down. The muscles don't really be tight, there'll be a lot of fat in the meat. The same thing with beef. You take a bear that's been scrapping for food—like in the swamps and eating gum berries and such—the meat is darker and tougher. I think it's because he works harder to get his food and he uses more muscle.

Sykes learned to tenderize the game's tough meat and neutralize its strong flavor.

You don't want to just take it in there and cook it. You want to soak it overnight if possible—get some of the blood out. Like I say, the blood is the key thing that makes the meat [taste] strong. There's a lot of little things you can do to make it better. You can put in a little bit of vinegar or lemon juice while it's soaking. You can add bay, thyme, onion, or garlic. Something stronger than what the scent of the animal is to eliminate some of the smell that's wild.

A lot of people put in a whole potato, wrap the potato in linen and tie it. It absorbs the musty odor from cooking the wild game. I seen my mom do that a lot of times. She'd take maybe a whole onion or a potato, and it would accumulate the odor from the strongest of the meat. That is one of the main keys to it, especially bear, because bear has a strong scent. Same thing with a buck deer that's been run by dogs; you want to really take time to make sure that you [get the scent out]. The key to it is boiling it slow and for a long time until it is tender. Same thing for the fowl, the goose, the swan, whatever you are preparing. You want to boil it a long time, and slow.

James Sykes' procedures for preparing venison are neither unique nor universal in this area. While he thinks boiling the meat is a prerequisite for frying or baking, other chefs prefer different techniques. Thelma Mooney of Shally Bags believes the game must be washed, but she sees no need to soak it or boil it before she dredges game in seasoned flour and drops it into hot grease. These different practices suggest the individual foodways of a culture linked to a hunting tradition.

Fully exploiting the wildlife resources available to them, the people of this region also served unconventional game. That squirrels, rabbits, deer, bear, ducks, geese, swans, quail, and dove often graced the supper table is not unusual. But reports of serving bullfrogs, turtles, possums, muskrats, otters, and raccoons are more novel. Local cooks even considered songbirds suitable for eating. James Sykes experimented with cooking a fox and a woodpecker, "just to see how it'd taste."

Bullfrogs were popular features on the menu. When he first started hunting frogs, Glynn Jarvis captured them for sale to a restaurant, but he acquired a taste for them himself.

> Ben Midgett, that run the cafe, he'd buy all the bullfrogs that the local boys caught. They'd dress them out and take him the legs and…he bought them by the pound, [and] served them in his restaurant. You could only catch the bullfrogs in the spring, but he would freeze them and have them on the menu year round. They were delicious! I remember the first ones that I caught…We sold some of them and Mama cooked some. They were *delicious*.

Maxine Simmons describes her husband's frogging technique:

> As long as Joe could walk he'd catch them with his hands. He'd get down in the ditch with a flashlight and put them in a bag and bring them home. He'd kill them and dress them that way. We'd fry the legs, and the families would get together and have great round platters of frogs legs—eighty or ninety pair.
>
> [After] he lost his leg, he'd take [his grandchildren] and here they'd go! We had a dog Cindy, who went with them. They'd gig the frog, or shoot it [with a .22], and Cindy would go overboard and retrieve it.

The ready abundance of turtles made them another local favorite. Thelma Mooney enjoyed turtles.

> Oh, yeah, I cooked turtles. I cooked turtles since I been here. I put all kinds of vegetables in it. We [caught a turtle] so big you could stand on its back and it'd walk. That big turtle was tough

to eat. Must have been a hundred years old.

Joe Simmons, renowned Hyde County hunting guide, learned a lot about turtle hunting from his Beaufort County friend and former neighbor, Jack Sykes. Sykes' wife taught Maxine Simmons how to prepare turtles for her husband.

> Nine out of ten people around the Lake wouldn't eat a turtle. We ate [turtle] because the Sykes ate it.
> You can stew it or you can fry it. After I got a pressure cooker I began to fry it—flour it, then brown it. Put water in the pressure cooker and it would make its own gravy. A big turtle wasn't as good as a small one. Joe liked his fried and cooked with gravy in it. He didn't like it crisp. If it was a female turtle and she had a lot of eggs in her—little round, soft shells—Joe liked them, too. I'd cook them for him.

Songbirds provided another source of food in Hyde and Tyrrell counties. William Cuthrell swears robins make an excellent meal, but because of their small size it takes between twenty-five and thirty to make an adequate stew. Maxine Simmons cooked robins with pastry. James Sykes has eaten robins but "did not care" for them. The meat "tasted too earthy," he recalled. "Tastes like an earthworm smells. In my family we'd try and catch them for a pet. Mom didn't recommend eating them too much. They ate too many earthworms."

Leslie Simmons III shows his size in relation to a snapping turtle; the turtle is one of several creatures captured by his father, Joe Simmons, in Hyde County.

Accepting wild game as a main dish is a distinguishing feature of this area. People who know how to prepare game and are familiar with it share a common ground. Frequently natives tell stories about finicky outsiders who express distaste for wild game, marking themselves as outlanders. When they unknowingly enjoy wild game they offer approval and support for the natives' traditional way of life. Thelma Mooney prepared a turtle stew for a relative who thanked her for "the best beef stew they'd ever had."

Edward "Bunk" Carawan tells a story about his father feeding venison to a man who swore he would not eat venison.

We had one fellow used to come down here from [Washington] D.C. He brought a man with him once that said the one thing he couldn't do is eat venison. They were staying at our house. My dad told my mother, he said, 'Don't say anything, just open a jar of that venison up and cook it tonight.' The best I remember we had some fish and stuff like that, and she had a mess of vegetables. But she fixed that half a gallon of venison. She put patties [potatoes] and onions in it, you know.

Went to eat that night [and] Daddy warned her not to say anything about 'pass the venison… [say] pass the beef.' That man got some of that "beef" and said, 'That's the best beef I've ever had in my life! What do you do to it?' My father was tickled, but he wouldn't say nothing. The guy said, 'I don't want to make a hog of myself, but I got to have another portion of that beef. It's the best beef I've ever had in my life!' [Laughs].

That night, they were sitting around playing checkers and [the man said], 'Mr. Carawan, I want to tell you one more time—I never eat no beef like that. That's the best I ever eat in my life.' My father said, 'Are you sure you enjoyed that beef?' 'Yes sir!' [Father] said, 'Well, I'm going to tell you, you say you can't eat venison, but tonight you're really full of venison.' [The man] couldn't believe it, so he asked my mother. She told him, 'Yeah, it was venison—some that I canned.' He told her, 'Next time I come down here fix some of it again. Don't tell me it's venison, but fix some of it.' [Laughs].

Working on the Water

Water surrounds and inundates Hyde County. The Pungo River marks its western boundary, and the Pamlico River defines the county's southern end. To the east, twenty miles of the Pamlico Sound separates the mainland from Ocracoke Island. Lake Mattamuskeet—the largest natural lake in the state—occupies approximately one hundred square miles of the county's center, and the impressive East Dismal Swamp controls the terrain in the north. Water regulates the geography and plays a profound role in shaping the region's traditions.

While sounds and swamps insulate the natives from mainstream society, the water also provides them with food and employment. In my travels, I talked with folks connected with three important maritime traditions: boat building, crabbing, and tying fishing nets. These keepers of traditions also adapt to new demands in order to compete in a keen market.

SCOTT TAYLOR

In addition to taking up the art of making decoys, Percy Carawan finds other ways to utilize his woodworking skills. His list of projects includes this boat that patiently awaits repair in his yard in Gull Rock, Hyde County.

Building Boats

Of all the manifestations of maritime material culture, few are as exciting or demanding as boat building. At one time, the skilled boat builder occupied an important position in any coastal community. Today, changes in technology, occupations, and transportation have all but pushed traditional boat builders out of the picture.

Robert Ross is one of Hyde County's last remaining traditional boat builders. Born in Swan Quarter in 1934, he never relied exclusively on boat building to earn a living. Like many people in Hyde County, he followed several occupations to make ends meet. Ross has operated a saw mill and a grist mill in partnership with his father. He has also repaired engines, crabbed, fished, trapped, and worked as a carpenter building houses and hunting blinds.

Ross began building boats with his father in the early 1950s as the older generation of boat builders dwindled. They built the boats for use in their fishing operation. "I'd build one and we'd use it. [We would] see the weak portions in it [and] we'd try to improve on it."

Ross consulted more experienced boat builders in his community—older men such as Joe Pugh in Gull Rock. Pugh used hand tools to build boats that ranged from small skiffs to thirty-footers. Besides showing Ross how to execute various cuts and angles, one of the best pieces of advice Pugh gave him was to exercise patience. He once told Ross:

> You're gonna fasten this board here and you're going to try and bend [it]. And you're going to bend it and bend it and pull it. About the time you have it shaped to where you want it, a couple of cracks are going to come in to it and it will pop and fly all to pieces. The only thing to do is go off, sit down and drink you a Coca-Cola. Let your nerves cool down. [Then] you can come back and do it next time!

Pugh's advice paid off. Working with his father, Ross started building skiffs and then graduated to more complex boats. The quality of his work attracted the attention of local watermen, and they asked Ross to build boats for them. As his reputation grew, the orders increased. Between 1953 and 1975, Ross estimates he built three hundred boats, skiffs, and prams. Hyde County native Mac Gibbs compares a boat built by Robert Ross to a luxury car. "When you had a Ross skiff, it's like having a Cadillac."

Ross did custom work for buyers. "They would tell me what they wanted. If somebody wanted a boat that was extra wide or extra narrow…that's what I built." Other boats he displayed on a roadside stand in hopes that a buyer would come along.

> A fourteen-foot boat would be the cheapest thing I could build out of cypress. I had the price as
> low as sixty-five dollars. That was about all I could cut on them…The boat—which was a fairly
> good line—would run you about $125, and you could do a little bit more to it. Some of the last
> boats I built in the early '70s I could sell…for about $300. That was an eighteen-foot boat built
> out of white cedar with gunwales and painted. To make it a little bit stronger I used salt-treated
> pine for the ribs. The same $300 boat, built using bronze hardware, would cost $400 or $425.
> Bronze was much better, although a good grade of American-made galvanized nails would last
> about ten years.

Robert Ross continued a venerable maritime tradition. By modifying his boats to meet the changing needs of the market, he extended the life of the tradition. Initially, he made boats for local people to use for working on the water and traveling. Ross' boats provided an affordable alternative to factory-made vessels. However, even when he began building boats, changes were already underway that would transform—and eventually end— the tradition as the market dried up. In the 1940s, military service and employment in defense industries lured many people away from Hyde County. Automobiles began replacing boats as highways and roads improved. In the 1960s, the need for working boats declined as fewer people looked to commercial fishing as an occupation.

Robert Ross realized that, although the demand for commercial fishing was waning, the interest in sport fishing was growing. The demand for small fishing boats increased as a result. Ross responded to the new trend. He switched from building boats and skiffs that local people kept moored near their homes, and turned to building smaller boats for sportsmen. "Folks who weren't local and didn't have a ditch to tie up their boat wanted a boat to move around and store in their yard," Ross explained. "A lot of people wanted a boat that could be taken out of the water and carried home."

In the mid-1960s he started building plywood boats "small enough to fit in the back of a pick-up truck." They sold like hotcakes. "I had an eight-foot pram-type which had a wide bow. That might not look like much more than a tub, but it was something a person could take and get around in those little ponds."

Robert Ross continued to build boats for the public until 1972. Declining demand and the difficulties of obtaining affordable, quality white cedar forced him to retire from this occupation. "The wood boat," Ross concedes, "was becoming extinct. Fiberglass is what's taking over."

As the market deteriorated, he turned to working on the water himself. Robert Ross made his last boats, as he had his first, for personal use. In the mid-1970s he built a twenty-foot work boat and an eighteen-foot plank skiff that he uses for crabbing. When one way of making a living evaporated, Ross turned to another in order to stay at home.

SCOTT TAYLOR

Robert Ross began building boats with his father in the early 1950s. He estimates that he built over 300 boats, skiffs and prams before he retired from the maritime profession in 1975.

Johnny Gibbs sorts live crabs caught in the Pamlico Sound by their size and sex.

SCOTT TAYLOR

Crabbing

Crabs play a big part in the diet and economy of this region. Seafood merchants buy the catch of local crabbers, and hire people to clean and pack the crabs for market. Twenty years ago African-American women filled this position. Now the work is performed almost exclusively by Mexican workers. Construction of crab pots—wire mesh boxes used to catch crabs—is a regional cottage industry.

In the spring and summer, it's common to see people standing on bridges or canal banks with a length of string and a dip net trying to snare crabs. A piece of bait tied to the end of the string attracts the crab. When the crab grabs the bait, it is pulled—still holding tightly to the bait—to within reach of the dip net. This method of crabbing works well in supplying a few crabs for supper, and resembles a small-scale version of the older commercial technique known as "trot lining" crabs.

Trot lines are long lengths of quarter-inch cotton rope. Bait—either pickled eel or scrap beef called "bull lip"—is attached to the line at four-foot intervals. The line is deployed in the sound and pulled to the surface as the crabs attack the bait.

Seth Bridgeman Credle began crabbing in the mid-1930s, and has vivid recollections of running trot lines.

The first time I ever went [crabbing], I wasn't nothing but a boy. You had about a mile of line. [If] you are running two lines, you'd put a half-mile on each line [with] an anchor and buoy on one end, and an anchor and buoy on the other. You used a piece of bull lip or eel about every four feet.

Drop an anchor and run that line on out 'till you come to the end. You had to get the line stretched just right so you could run the line over a little roller that would bring your crabs to the top. You'd do all your lines that way—had to be just right. Then come back with your boat. You got a roller sticking off the side of the boat. Put the line on that roller and go along, and the crab will come to the roller. The roller will kick the crab in the net. [Laughs].

It's pretty, too, watching them crabs when the line's coming over that little roller. Sometimes there'd be two crabs to the bait. It'd just charm you to see how they'd hold on."

Despite the hard work, Seth Credle enjoyed running trot lines.

George Edward Bush was not a trot line fan. "I tried it for three or four days," he recalled, "and it was just stinking to me. That old bull lip, you could smell it for half a mile. And the flies!" Bush farmed in Hyde County's New Holland community. After a series of hurricanes destroyed his crops in 1954, he turned to working on the water and taking in some goose hunters to earn money. A visiting goose hunter from Manns Harbor noticed Bush's struggle with trot lines and suggested that he try crab pots instead. Bush had never seen a crab pot, so the hunter brought one and explained how to use it. "Don't know where he got it. That was the beginning."

It was a beginning, indeed. Using the Manns Harbor pot as a model, Bush and his wife, Geraldine, began making their own. In the process, they revolutionized crabbing in Hyde County and coastal North Carolina. Using a board, a hammer, and a pair of pliers, they cut and folded lengths of chicken wire into two "U" shapes. The two shaped pieces of wire were joined together to form a cube. A wire divider inserted between the two sections separated them into an "upstairs" and a "downstairs." Bait placed inside the pot's wire basket attracted the crabs, which would then enter the trap through round tunnels of wire. Geraldine Bush used bent nails and coat hanger wire to hold the pieces of the pot together.

Initially, they made nine pots and George Bush set them in a reed bank of the Out Fall Canal near their home. The crab pots caught an unbelievable four hundred pounds of crabs. "That beat all! I ain't never seen that much since then. They just filled the inside up and they were hanging on the outside. There were so many blamed crabs they couldn't even eat the bait what was in there. [Laughs]. That was the first crab pots ever been put in that sound."

The crab pots greatly improved George Bush's profits, attracted the attention of other watermen, and opened business opportunities for Geraldine. When a good friend asked about crab pots, the Bushes came to his aid and instructed him on how to assemble a pot. Soon the friend called for help. "Can you build them pots for me?" he asked. "I'll tell you the truth, our fingers are so sore we can't even scratch!" Another waterman witnessed Bush's success and requested crab pots, too. "Build me some of those things. I'll have me some [crab pots] if they cost one hundred dollars! You're making twice as much money as me and ain't fighting half the flies."

As more and more watermen called upon the Bush household for crab pots, Geraldine took the lead in the manufacturing enterprise. Production grew to meet the demands. At its height, Bush's Crab Pot Shop employed sixteen workers. Under Geraldine's guidance, her family developed more efficient ways to make crab pots. A chicken farmer in Virginia suggested that she use a "cutting arm" to trim wire to the right length. A furniture upholsterer inspired the use of power tools for stapling the pots together and cutting the trap's entrance. Originally a board and a hammer were the tools used to fold the lengths of wire into the proper shapes for the crab pot. Geraldine credits her son with devising the "folding table" now used to bend the wire.

Bush's Crab Pot Shop has made a significant contribution to this area's heritage. The shop supplied crab pots to watermen from Virginia to South Carolina. In 1968 the Bushes moved to Oak Hill, Florida, and introduced crab pots to that part of the country. They have since returned to North Carolina. Geraldine's operation perfected some of the techniques used in crab pot manufacture. She has instructed some of Hyde County's leading crab pot makers. Bush apprentices include Mary Helen Cox of Fairfield, and Elaine Mayo of Scranton. Observing

George and Geraldine Bush pause in front of their Fairfield, Hyde County workshop. They began making crab pots in the early 1960s.

SCOTT TAYLOR

the dissemination of the crab pot in coastal North Carolina offers a striking example of the folk process at work.

Elaine Mayo heads Mayo's Commercial Fishing Supply. She employs twenty-five people, and uses power tools to manufacture more than 40,000 crab pots a year. Because of this industrialized, high-volume production, Mayo does not see herself as a member of a folk community. A closer examination of her occupation reveals its strong ties to tradition. Her most obvious link to folk culture is the informal way she learned to make crab pots. "A neighbor showed me how to make them." Her crab pot plant makes a specialized product that responds to the needs of a community of watermen. She "speaks" the language of crabbers, and builds pots to suit them.

On the other hand, Mary Helen Cox has no doubt about her position in the folk community. An invitation to demonstrate crab and eel pot making for the North Carolina Museum of History validated her place in the community of watermen. Mary Helen joined that community as a pot maker in 1980 when Geraldine Bush invited her to participate. Cox could earn money and watch her young children at the same time. When Bush retired, Cox went solo. "I knew enough and knew most of the customers, and felt I could make a go of it."

Cox's establishment is small. She employs four other people. The folding table and cutting arm she uses to assemble crab pots differs from Geraldine Bush's contraption only in that it is hydraulically powered. She sells her pots as far south as Wilmington, and as far north as Virginia.

Cox adjusts her product to meet the demands of her customers. The cheapest pot uses non-galvanized chicken wire, but most commercial crabbers choose pots made of a heavier gauge wire protected by a thick plastic coating. The plastic coating comes in different colors, and some crabbers believe that the color of the plastic affects their catch. Based on her customers' requests, she manufactures crab pots in a variety of colors.

Although crab pots are the biggest part of her business, Cox has also made "pots" for catching fish, eels, crawfish and "peelers." Peelers are crabs in the process of shedding their hard exoskeleton and becoming desirable "soft crabs." "Anything a man out there on that water comes up with…" Cox boasts, "I'll manage to make for him."

Making eel pots is more complex than making crab pots. The crab pot is square, while eel pots are round. Installing cloth tunnels that funnel eels into the trap consumes most of the time. In the time it takes Cox to make one eel pot, she can make four crab pots. Because only live eels are sold, Cox also manufactures large wire pens to hold them underwater until the buyer picks them up. She jokingly refers to these pens as "caskets," because of their size, shape, and the difficulty of making them.

She enjoys making peeler pots and calls them "the prettiest work in this business." Pots for catching "peelers" are specially designed crab pots made from soft galvanized chicken wire. A peeler pot has a specially constructed cage for holding sexual bait, because a male crab (a "hot jimmy") is used to entice female peelers into the trap. "Sometimes the she-crabs are clinging to the outside of the pots when the pots are pulled in," Cox observes. "Talk about a fool for love!"

Like Elaine Mayo and Mary Helen Cox, Robert Ross learned to make crab pots from George and Geraldine

SCOTT TAYLOR

Geraldine Bush demonstrates how crab pots are made using a specially constructed folding table.

SCOTT TAYLOR

Mary Helen Cox learned to make crab pots from Geraldine Bush. Using power tools and several helpers, she manufactures thousands of crab pots each year.

Bush. Rather than sell the pots, he uses them for his own crabbing enterprise. "I try and make them in the coldest, worst part of the winter," he explaines, "the time of the year when there's nothing else to do."

Ross' description of using crab pots makes it easy to understand why people abandoned trot lines. Placing bait in a crab pot's "bait cage" is much simpler and faster than attaching each individual piece of bait to the trot line. Trot lines also require caution and constant attention to catch crabs. If the trot lines are not handled carefully, the crabs will release the bait and escape. On the other hand, crab pots can be deployed and checked at the crabber's convenience. Because crab pots can be left unattended, people can work at other jobs and crab on the side.

> [T]here is some that crab different ways. A lot of the part-timers have a job. Maybe they get off at 4:30 or 5:00. Well, in the summertime, at 5:00, you still got three or four hours of daylight. Some of them will crab a few pots in the morning before they go to work. If they go to work at 8:00, the sun's up a long time before 8:00. [T]hey got them some pots and they will go out there and add to their income.
>
> [Crab pots are set] anywhere in the open water…there are crabs one place then another. Used to be finding a place where there is a lot of shells indicated a good area [to catch crabs]. A lot of it is trial and error. Crabbers will put out what they call sample pots or spotter pots [to locate crabs]. After the pots are out, you check them every other day until the catch picks up and justifies checking them every day.
>
> Some years you catch them in April, some years it's May before you get any. Everybody is racing to catch those early crabs, which bring a good price.

In late spring when crabbing season is in full swing, Ross puts out between 200 and 300 pots in locations likely to yield crabs. He drops a baited pot off his boat, and it sinks to the bottom of the sound. A line attaches a buoy to the crab pot and it floats on the surface, marking the pot's location. When he checks his catch, he approaches the line of buoys and uses a winch—a "pot puller"—to hoist the pot to the boat. Ross describes the process: "I pull the pot up, dump the old bait out, and shake the crabs into a box. Then I re-bait the pot and use it to replace the next pot. Sometimes the pot is empty, and sometimes it has ten pounds of crabs. But ten pounds is a big catch, almost a thing of the past. Usually it averages two to three pounds per pot."

Ross enjoys crabbing. He likes being out on the water and the surprise of discovering what he has caught. He also has a keen appreciation of crabbing's economics. "You want the work to justify the expense," Ross says. "[You] don't want to come home with a sore back and sore arms and empty crab pots. You don't get paid for a day's work, and that gets old real quick."

BILL MANSFIELD

Geraldine Moran uses a converted house trailer as a net shop.

Making Nets

The advent of the crab pot added another layer of tradition to the waterman's occupation. Likewise, the introduction of mass-produced monofilament webbing changed the tradition of making fishing nets. Before the availability of mass-produced monofilament webbing, fishing nets were tied by hand in a complex, time-consuming process. Crafting the net took a great deal of labor, as did maintaining the net after its completion. The natural cotton fiber of the net twine absorbed water, adding weight to a net and making it necessary to dry the net after use. Compared to cotton, monofilament is stronger, lighter, and less expensive. It is also easier to use and requires less maintenance. Not surprisingly, the manufactured synthetic nets quickly replaced the older, hand-tied nets.

The prevalence of manufactured webbing eliminates the need for those skilled in tying nets. Today people with that knowledge are rare. Gaston Saddler is one of them. Born in the Rose Bay community of Hyde County, Saddler began fishing with his father in the early 1930s. He learned to tie nets at home and describes the process simply as "work."

> You make you a gauge out of wood [to measure the size of the net's marsh]. Then, how ever many marshes deep you want that net, you go ahead and tie that many off. Then you tie a string through the marshes, and put them together. Then you start making the length of it. You'd tie it in the house at night, when you wasn't fishing or working on the water. It takes a long time to finish one. You just sit there and tie them, you don't do nothing else while you tie them.

The use of industrial monofilament webbing transformed, but did not end the tradition of making fishing nets. Geraldine Moran of Tyrrell County's River Neck community is part of this changing tradition. Moran was born in 1939, and her mother taught her the craft. Moran attaches the monofilament webbing to the ropes that support it and give it shape, turning it into a net. She calls this process "hanging nets." "Mother just strung it up and told me to try it. I tried it and caught right on. I was about thirteen years old when I started. Been hanging ever since."

Now Moran is aware of the traditional nature of her craft, and hopes it will continue in her family. "[Hanging nets] was handed down from generation to generation. [Mother] taught me, and now I'm teaching my daughter. She can hang [nets], tie her knots, and maybe she can hand it down to her kids."

Though Moran "ties" the webbing to the ropes, she prefers the term "hanging nets," which aptly describes the

SCOTT TAYLOR

Patricia Roughten (left) attaches the "cork" or top line to a fishing net while Geraldine Moran (right) secures the bottom line.

procedure. She works with her friend and business partner, Patricia Roughton, in a house-trailer converted to a net shop. The interior walls of the trailer have been removed to provide a long work space. Two wooden rectangular frames stand about thirty feet apart. From one side of the frame hangs the top line of a net, and the bottom line hangs from the other side. In between the top and bottom lines Moran strings the "mark line." As its name implies, the "mark line" is measured off and marked at regular intervals to indicate where to tie the knots that attach the webbing to the lines. Several "mark lines" are stored in their shop, each one measured for a different type of net. As Moran says, "Every net is different. [Where you tie the marsh] depends on the kind of webbing they bring, and the kind of net they want."

Moran attaches the webbing to the bottom line of the net, while Roughton joins the webbing to the top line.

> We have what you call a top line and a bottom line. She [Roughton] works on the top line with the corks. I work on what they call the lead line—the [weighted] bottom line. She has to put corks on this line every twenty yards.
>
> It is easier if you got two people hanging than if it is just one. If one is hanging, you got to do this and then run around and do the next line, then take it up all by yourself and start over. Working in pairs is better, because when one gets out the other is finished. It is a whole lot faster.

Fishermen supply Moran and Roughton with all the materials required for the net. They obtain the webbing, lines, weights, and floats from fishing supply houses. While it might appear that using mass-produced materials to assemble a fishing net would produce a unified product, this is not the case. Variations in the craftsmanship of assembling a net can make all the difference in the world. "If you ain't got the net hung right," Moran explains, "they're not going to catch."

Apparently the nets Geraldine Moran and Patricia Roughton make are hung right. Fishermen come from as far away as Wanchese on Roanoke Island to ask Moran and Roughton to hang their nets—and their reputation is spreading. "We got five new customers this year from Wanchese," Moran commented. "This coming year we may have ten new customers." As Moran suggests, a traditional culture does not exist apart from an economic culture. All too often, tradition-bearers are presented as benevolent keepers of community wisdom when, in fact, they are active participants in a competitive market.

Robert Ross changed his construction techniques to meet a changing market and gave up building boats when his market disappeared. The Bushes tell a story of a rival crab pot maker disconnecting their telephone in an effort to drive them out of business. Geraldine Bush expresses regret for allowing people to tour her workshop and copy her innovations. Once she attempted to patent her ideas, but by the time she applied for the patent, her designs had already become part of the crab pot "tradition."

Geraldine Moran wants her family to carry on the tradition, but has no interest in teaching anyone else.

> If you're teaching everybody else then you're cutting your own throat. In this job, the least you have that knows how [to hang nets], the better off you are. They ain't many that knows how, and that way more people are going to come to you. If you're out here teaching everybody, that's some more that you're teaching that'll cut your throat. I taught one [and] now she is in it on her own, too. She don't get as many [customers] as we do, but she is in it [hanging nets]. After that I said I ain't teaching nobody else.

Boats, crab pots and fishing nets are traditional parts of the waterman's material culture—as well as tools in his economic inventory. Robert Ross, Geraldine Bush, and Geraldine Moran are traditional craftspeople in the way they learned their craft, the way they practice their craft, and in the way they serve a community of watermen. While it is important to recognize their place as artisans in the maritime tradition, it is equally important to recognize their place as entrepreneurs in the maritime economy.

Social Life

SCOTT TAYLOR

Edward "Bunk" Carawan earned the reputation as a talented square dance caller, a skill he learned while playing for dances all across Hyde County.

Making Music

Informal, community-based music—also called folk music, traditional music, or vernacular music—is still heard in this region, but you must listen carefully. Outside of church-related events, homemade music has all but vanished from the cultural landscape. When people gather to worship they still make their own music, but in the past thirty years, radios and CD players have replaced musicians at secular events. Nonetheless, homemade music is still found in the privacy of the home rather than in public places. Indeed, the most enduring musical tradition here is not any one particular genre, but the tradition of making music itself.

Though presently suffering, vernacular secular music enjoyed a healthy past. Older members of the community—both black and white—tell many stories about local musicians and public performances. Their recollections give a good picture of a once-vibrant musical community.

Cadwell Bowser remembers. Born in 1907, Bowser ran a juke joint in Columbia. He has vivid recollections of Hyde County musician Manual Morris performing on the guitar and harmonica. "He'd get a crowd up out on the street listening at him. He used to sing that piece about 'The Traveling 'Coon.'" The presence of this song in Morris' repertoire links him with an older, pre-blues tradition. Hannah Mackey of Engelhard also recalls Morris providing music at juke joints and pie suppers.

Born in 1910 in Pamlico Beach, banjo player David Hopkins remembers the first time he heard a black man, Elijah Brown, perform in a Hyde County lumber camp in 1917.

> He was a playing man. He picked the guitar with his fingers, and he could play so plain he could make it talk. He could play 'Nearer My God to Thee' so plain you could hear the younguns a-crying in there. He was the playingest man I ever heared in this world. And sing! Just like a bird. Music would just roll out of his mouth. I can't decide which was better, his singing or playing.

About this time, Hopkins began playing the banjo. His older brother gave him the instrument and enough instruction to get him started. He plays the banjo using a simple two-finger style. Picking the melody on the first four strings with his index finger, he uses his thumb to play drone notes on the fifth string. He didn't play for many dances, but he made music around the house with his brother-in-law Burl Foster, who played the fiddle.

Arthur Bryant, an eighty-nine-year-old African-American from Tyrrell County, enjoyed a reputation as a skilled harmonica player.

I could do anything in the world with a mouth harp I wanted to. Blowed a mouth harp so well the white man at the lumber commissary nicknamed me "DeFord Bailey" [after the harmonica virtuoso on WSM's Grand Ole Opry]. White people'd hire me to blow the mouth harp, and buy me liquor to play. They would get out there and dance and have a lot of fun. Everybody had something to drink. The drunker I got the better I'd play. I could get a free drunk anytime I wanted just by playing for the white people. They loved to hear that music. I could blow any kind of blues.

Bryant played for parties with a guitarist named Jerry Measure. "He could play anything he wanted. He could sing, too—any type of blues." Bryant taught several of his black neighbors and a few interested white people how to blow a mouth harp. He spent two years working and living with Dallas Smith, a white farmer and his family. In that time the Smiths taught him to play the banjo. "I could pick it with my fingers or knock it with my fist. When I was young I could catch songs fast." Unfortunately, old age has taken its toll. Arthur Bryant no longer has the breath to play the mouth harp, and a stroke has deprived him of the use of his left hand.

Born in 1914, Swan Quarter native Edward Cuthrell began learning the guitar in the early 1920s. He received some lessons from local guitarist Maxwell Carawan, but learned more playing in a string band. "Macon Spencer of Rose Bay played fiddle, and Cecil Saddler played banjo. They had a wonderful time playing, and provided music for any occasion that called for it. They took me under their wing, showed me about chords and chord changes and playing in different keys. They helped me a lot."

His older brother Elbert learned to "pick the banjo and knock it a little, too" from neighbor Carroll Midgett. The Cuthrell brothers joined with mandolin player Fred Tunnell and guitarist Frank Harris to make music. The sounds of other local musicians, as well as bands heard on radio station WSM's Grand Ole Opry—whose music differed little from that heard in the community—influenced their band. They often made music for neighborhood square dances.

Back then times were hard, and entertainment hard to come by. A lot of times we held dances in people's homes. They would peel the carpet back on the floor and we'd start playing. We had a real good time.

There wouldn't be any great big crowd, [because] back then they didn't have any way of letting it be known. It was just the neighborhood. On average there would be seven or eight couples dancing. There were several who could call the figures. I'd call 'em if I got a chance to dance.

Rufus Carawan was a great old-time dancer. He was liable to ask you to play a good fast piece and he'd fall out in the floor and clog dance for you—even when he was way up in his sixties! He could dance, too! The dancers didn't really stomp their feet [but] it would get a little noisy at times.

Abraham Cahoon's store was vacant and available for dances. They danced there right often. They'd walk over to the store and we'd play and sing 'till ten-thirty or eleven o'clock. It was a lot of fun.

When asked to recollect square dance figures, everyone interviewed described a similar set of uncomplicated calls. Edward "Bunk" Carawan earned a reputation as a talented caller, a skill he learned while playing for the dances in a string band. Carawan called "from the floor"—that is, he led the couples through the figures while participating in the square dance himself.

A crowd of people would get on the floor and you'd always start out with, 'Hands around!' Everybody'd join hands and go around in a circle. Then you'd call, 'Take partner by the right hand and go right and left, all the way through, 'till you got back around to your partner and swing her.

When everybody got through you'd say, 'Promenade!' Then you'd go around in a circle and say, 'First couple lead off with four hands around.' At that, the dancers would pair off into sets of four. Everybody would do that.

You'd call, 'Hands across,' then, 'Birdie in the nest.' One dancer would get in the center while the others circled around. Then came 'Birdie fly out, and the chicken fly in' and the person in the center changes. Then, 'You swing mine and I'll swing yours.'

After running through the figures you'd move on to another couple. Everybody had a chance to dance with everybody else. Sometimes you'd wind up the ball of yarn and the younger folks liked to rush to the center. When you saw everyone getting tired you'd say, 'Honor your partner' [and end the dance].

Usually the calls "wind up the ball of yarn" or "rush to the center" ended the dance and, ironically, overturned the orderly patterned figures of the dance. To "wind up the ball of yarn" Carawan had the dancers join hands and led them around in a twisting, choreographed version of "crack-the-whip." When Carawan called "rush to the center," the dancers—circling single file—charged towards the center of the circle defined by the dance, ending the set with a good-natured collision.

Musicians needed no special reason to play, and often gathered for their own enjoyment. H. Ray Modlin, from Yeatsville in eastern Beaufort County, describes a common occurrence.

Every chance you got, you'd just pick up your instruments and walk to your buddy's house, or he'd come and see you. Two or three would get together and some times we'd stay all night. All of us would sleep on the floor, then we'd get up, fix our breakfast, and stay around the house and play all day the next day until late in the afternoon. We enjoyed playing. The more you do it, the more you like it.

Modlin recalls playing music with brothers Ray and Ralph Osborne; "one played guitar and the other blowed the mouth harp and played clawhammer banjo." He fondly remembers Mac Lilly. "We'd play with him every time we could find him because he played real good guitar and sang real good." Neighbor and good friend Julian Elliot played mandolin and sang tenor to Modlin's lead vocals. They emulated performers they heard on the radio, and were particularly taken by the sound of the "brother duets" so popular in the 1930s and '40s. Neighbor Darryl Leggit often added his fiddle to the music.

When friends and relatives danced the musicians rarely charged, but playing for strangers was another matter. Modlin, Elliot and Leggit picked up extra money at square dances. His story of a paid performance is quite similar to—yet very different from—Edward Cuthrell's account of dances. Cuthrell played for fun among friends and neighbors; Modlin provided dance music for paying customers.

We played at a lot of these dances at old pack houses where people used to grade their tobacco. They'd clean [the pack house] up for a Saturday night dance. Most of the time they'd start about dark—around six or six-thirty—and have kerosene lamps. They'd have a place for us to stand, but sometimes it was kind of a small area.

I know we weren't over fifteen years old. I think we played 'till two or three in the morning. The man we played for carried us home in his truck. Our parents didn't say anything. They knew we were all right as long as we had our instruments with us. They knew what we were doing.

People carried money in the front pocket of bib overalls. [They] would give us a dollar, but they didn't mind that, and everybody went in just to have a good time. They'd have somebody to call the sets. We'd get with him and just start playing. They really enjoyed it, and would dance all night if you stayed there and played for them.

Fiddlers' conventions presented an opportunity for musicians to visit and share music, as well as to win prestige and a little money. Edward Cuthrell remembers schools and civic organizations raising funds by sponsoring fiddlers' conventions. The audience paid a small admission fee and listened to bands and soloists compete. Judges evaluated the musicians and awarded prizes for the best performances. "We never won any prizes," Cuthrell recalls, "but our band came in second a lot of times. We could hold our own." The competition came from fiddlers Robey Fulcher, James Ambrose, Ace Hamilton, and banjo player Hack Lamb. Any member of the Carawan family proved to be fierce competition as well.

The Carawan Family enjoyed a reputation for good music in this region. Patriarch Rufus Carawan danced, played the fiddle, "knocked" the banjo, and created an atmosphere that encouraged his children's musical talent. They all sang, and most of them became proficient on several stringed instruments. Emmett played the mandolin and fiddle; Maxwell played the guitar, fiddle and banjo; and Willfred played the banjo and guitar. Seth and Gyon played the fiddle.

Maxwell Carawan taught his children, John, Maxwell Jr., and Earl to play. They often joined him at fiddlers' conventions and square dances. The Carawans also played for radio broadcasts on Washington radio station WRRF. John recalled that his father used every opportunity to further his music. Maxwell Carawan drove a "rolling store" for merchants in Belhaven. This general store on the back of a truck carried commodities to customers living in the country.

> We'd get a lot of gigs because we were on the truck. We run all over Hyde County. You know, people wanting to dance, or they wanted something for school entertainment—cake walks and things to raise a little money for whatever they was trying to pay for. We got a lot of little gigs around to the schools and stuff all over the county.

The dance site best remembered by Hyde County's older white residents is Barber Shanty, a dance pavilion in the Lake Landing community. Sam Barber opened the place in 1933, and until it closed in 1957, Barber Shanty hosted weekly dances. The community of local musicians performed there.[2] "We were all in and out playing," John Carawan recalls. "So whoever could play that night, that's who played."

The story of Barber Shanty presents a clear example of a culture in transition. The recollections of a woman who attended weekly dances in the mid-1930s as a teenager provide a clear picture of the older folk culture's shift towards popular culture.

"Oh man, everybody had a good time and everybody was there. A lot of the parents went, and a lot of the older people went and just stood around and observed." These adults chaperoned the dance (preserving order) and instructed the dancers (preserving traditions). "There were some older men who taught us how to square dance. They were tall and they would just reach over and take you by the hand and lead you around."

However, the older traditions could not prevail when they confronted technology and the power of popular

---

2 Among the list of musicians who performed for the dances were: fiddle-Seth Carawan, Gyon Carawan, James Ambrose, Herman Swindell; banjo-Willfred Carawan, John Carawan, Elbert Cuthrell; guitar-Maxwell Carawan, Earl Carawan, Edward Cuthrell, Herman Parks, Earl Edwards; mandolin-Edward Carawan, Fred Tunnell; piano-Nat Williams, Oliver Boomer; accordion-Billy Williams.

SCOTT TAYLOR

An abandoned gas station and snack bar stands on the site of Hyde County's Barber Shanty dance pavilion, which closed in 1957.

culture. Barber Shanty not only hosted a string band for square dancing, but also had a juke box for "modern dancing." Music from the juke box opened the dances—before the band started—and provided music for the "jitterbugs" between square dances. A regular participant at the dances, the same woman reminisces:

> A man would come from Greenville every Thursday afternoon and he changed the records in that juke box. We would go down there and dance while he changed the records. If we had a special record we liked, we'd get him to leave it on the juke box.
>
> We danced to 'Three Little Fishes in the Itty Biddy Pool,' 'Deep Purple,' 'Harbor Lights,' and 'Chattanooga Choo Choo'—mostly Guy Lombardo, Tommy Dorsey, and Glenn Miller.

This story reveals how popular music and mass culture affected community-based vernacular music. The fact that she was a regular at the dances and has no strong recollections of the string band's music, yet vivid memories of specific artists and records from the juke box, suggests how popular commercial music replaced the older traditions.

The shift from community-based vernacular music to mainstream commercial music occurred in the African-American community as well. The musical career of Gerald Lee Bryant exemplifies this change. Born in Engelhard in 1944, Bryant's earliest musical memories are of his mother's harmonica. "She could blow it and play some beautiful music. That's what made me play the guitar. I really had a love for music."

In the early 1950s Bryant began learning the guitar. He picked up some lessons from John Carawan, a white friend known for country music. However, the music of William Martin—a black man from Belhaven—had a greater influence on his musical development.

> He come down here to open oysters. They had a house for the men that opened oysters to stay in. I'd go up there every now and then. He had an electric guitar and a little amplifier to go with it. He was always playing. He could play guitar and blow a mouth harp. Had a bar [rack] he'd set the mouth harp on. He'd put a glass on his finger and slide on the guitar with that. I liked it so good! Every now and then he'd come down to my house and play. He was teaching me.

Bryant's recollections suggest that Martin's repertoire spanned African-American musical styles—from pre-blues to rhythm and blues.

> He played right by hisself. He played a lot of them old songs. I wouldn't call them hillbilly, but… folk songs that people just put together. He played one song:

SCOTT TAYLOR

From R&B to soul and funk, Gerald Lee Bryant's music changed to keep pace with the changing expectations of his audience.

[Sings]

'I had a girl name of Sue, she shore knew what to do. Old Uncle John and old Aunt Sally jumped back in the alley.'

He played that 'C.C. Rider' and 'Lawdey Lawdey Miss Claudie.' People would dance [to his music]. Back then the old folks had all kinds of dances. They had the rabbit dance, square dance, the huckle-buck, and the camel walk—all kinds of dances.

As he grew older Bryant visited juke joints in his area. The music he heard there replaced the older style of music learned from William Martin.

A lot of times [juke joints] had guys going around playing guitars. They'd charge so much to get in. This is the way I was learning how to play, by watching them.

A cousin of mine, Henry Spencer, started bringing some bands down from Norfolk, Virginia. [The band] had two guitars, a bass player, and a drummer—sort of like blues. I started trying to play like those guys.

Attracted by this music and eager to learn, Bryant studied this band and continued his informal training. "I learnt by watching the way the band from Virginia was doing." Occasionally, the band borrowed his amplifier, and this gave Bryant the chance to "sit in" with them. Eventually he formed his own ensemble with Lewis Mann on guitar, Thurman Shelton playing drums, Elbert Lee Spencer singing, and Bryant on bass. The group began performing and—under Bryant's direction—adapted their sound to meet audience expectations. "Learn all the latest songs. If you can play the latest songs, play it right and they can dance to it, then [the audience] ain't going to leave you."

The band went through a number of personnel and stylistic transformations to keep pace with changing trends. They started out playing rhythm and blues music inspired by Chuck Berry. When soul and funk music became popular in the late 1960s, Bryant recruited some music students from Elizabeth City State University, and added a horn section to the band. They began to pattern their music after James Brown. Called the "Easy Funk Connection," Bryant's group performed in Hyde and Tyrrell counties, as well as other regional venues, before disbanding in the mid-1970s.

The band dissolved for several reasons. The strain of performing and working full-time jobs, conflicts within the band, the long trips required to get to gigs in the scattered small towns of northeastern North Carolina— all of these factors took their toll. Disco music proved to be the ultimate blow. DJs spinning records satisfied the public, and club owners no longer needed live performers.

Gerald Lee Bryant's story of how local music changed under the influence of popular styles represents the story of vernacular music everywhere. Secular vernacular music slowly disappeared in the African-American community. "Bowser's Place," a juke joint in Columbia, never hosted live musicians. "Cookies," a juke joint located in Tyrrell County's Gum Neck community, closed down years ago. So did the "Hill Top" and "Sugar Shack," both in Hyde County. Only "Blount's Play Ground," in Hyde County's Gull Rock community, remains open. Today however, a juke box and a DJ provide the music in this public arena.

The white community has also seen areas for public performance fade away. After Barber Shanty closed in 1957, a few venues for local performers remained. In Fairfield, there was "Gene's Roof Top Garden." The "Popperinia" and the "Sound Side," both located in Engelhard, furnished a stage for musicians, but they closed in the mid-1970s. Despite the demise of these establishments, community music sessions featuring local musicians continued. Glynn Jarvis combined fish fries and music sessions for friends and neighbors at his Oyster Creek Marina. Warren Williams scheduled weekly music sessions after business hours in his Swan Quarter store. These venues gave many of the Barber Shanty musicians a place to perform.

Today, secular vernacular music has all but disappeared from the public and from the community. Where it does exist, it exists in the privacy of the home. The Carawan brothers still get together for music in Hyde County. In Beaufort County, H. Ray Modlin—who passed his love of music on to his sons—joins them for bluegrass music. In the Tyrrell County community of Killkenny, Edison

BILL MANSFIELD

Fred Blount opened his juke joint, Blount's Play Ground, in the late 1940s, when such places abounded in Hyde County; it's the only one remaining. It still serves as a gathering place for the county's Gull Rock community.

Cahoon continues the musical tradition of his family by singing old ballads learned at home. He sings old favorites like 'The Knoxville Girl' and 'Barbara Allen,' as well as more recent narrative songs like 'Old Shep' and 'The Death of Hank Williams.'

If *secular* vernacular music languishes, *sacred* vernacular music flourishes. It fills a need, and the church community provides a supportive audience.

Performance venues abound for sacred music. Many churches minister to the region, and their regularly scheduled services require music from the congregation—in most cases, a choir. Many churches sponsor several choirs that range in age from "youth" to "senior adult." In addition, church-related activities provide a stage and an audience for sacred music. Homecomings, revivals, church suppers, fund-raisers, outreach ministries, and church pageants all create occasions for musical performance. Frequently, families host celebrations in their church. Reunions, important birthdays, and anniversaries offer more opportunities for musical performance.

Community concerts also feature performances of sacred music. In Tyrrell County many churches participate in "Singspirations." Every fifth Sunday in the month, people gather to sing hymns and to enjoy the performance of choirs from different area churches. The location rotates among participating congregations. The Riverside Campground in Hyde County also offers concerts of sacred music every Saturday night.

The many opportunities for performance have spawned quite a few sacred ensembles. Some of these groups are based in congregations, yet receive no official church sponsorship. The "Southern Gospel Aires" is an example of such a group. The members attend Hyde County's Pleasant Grove Church of God and unite to sing "southern gospel music." "The Happy Followers" of Gum Neck in Tyrrell County is a family ensemble. Brothers "JC" and Burvel Jones, along with Burvel's wife Barbara, perform at every opportunity. The members of "The Sons of God"—an African-American gospel group—live in four separate counties. In spite of the miles between them, they come together to sing songs of praise.

The friendly, family-oriented atmosphere nurtures the artists. The audience takes for granted the good intentions of the musicians, and accepts all levels of performance ability. They also tolerate a wide range of musical styles. Archaic a cappella singing and contemporary gospel music accompanied by "soundtrack" tapes are welcomed with equal enthusiasm.

The camaraderie of these venues gives performers a safe and supportive environment where they can develop and maintain their art. The story of gospel musician James T. Bryant illustrates this point. James is consumed by music, and sacred song provided a healthy outlet for his creative energies.

> I always wanted to play guitar. When I was a kid, I tore pictures [of guitars] out of order books
> and carried them around in my pocket so I could look at them. Playing music is the first thing I
> do in the morning, and the last thing I do at night. Sometimes I wake up at three or four o'clock

SCOTT TAYLOR

Trucks speed past the site of Hyde County's Barber Shanty on Highway 264.

in the morning and start playing.

I wanted to play blues and rock. I was in the devil's field — going from night club to night club, house parties, and holes in the wall. There was drinking and shooting. People got mad with you 'cause all the girls start hollering when you start playing. The devil's work was killing me. I just got tired. I turned to Jesus. With Jesus you don't need nothing to make you high. You're already high.

Not all accounts are as dramatic as James Bryant's, but others have turned from secular to sacred music. Jerome Bryant, guitarist with "The Sons of God," enjoyed playing soul and funk music with a local band. As a more mature man, he appreciates gospel music because it gives him "the chance to serve God, play music, and get home to my family at a decent hour."

Sacred vernacular music flourishes in this region because the need still exists. Audiences hunger for sacred music, and people want to express their faith through song. Recordings cannot replace the immediacy and sincerity of people expressing their devotion with music.

Secular vernacular music is another story. A number of factors account for its decline. Technology helped replace community music. Not only did recordings supplant live music, they introduced other diversions. More than one person interviewed for this project stated that homemade music played a prominent part in their lives because "there wasn't anything else to do." Radio, television, videos, computer games, and the Internet all compete for leisure time. Improved roads and the availability of automobiles permit people to seek entertainment outside the region.

The dwindling population of Hyde and Tyrrell counties also contributes to declining musical traditions. Several people commented on the shrinking population of the region, and census figures bear them out.[3] As people pass away or pass out of the counties, the audience that supports vernacular secular music contracts — as does the number of potential musicians to maintain the tradition. Commenting on the operation of his juke joint, Cadwell Bowser stated, "There wasn't enough people here to support one juke joint, not to mention four." With no audience to perform for and no younger musicians replacing the retiring musicians, it's no surprise that secular vernacular music is in decline.

Though musical traditions contract, they also endure. Churches provide a stage and audience for sacred community music; private homes and family reunions are the settings for secular music.

---

3 Hyde County's population has declined by more than 3,000 people since 1930. Tyrrell County's already sparse population shrank by more than 1, 500 in the same period of time. (Daw: 1990:4).

BILL MANSFIELD

William and Etta Mae Cuthrell display a partially completed quilt outside of their home in Killkenny, Tyrrell County.

Quilting Traditions

Most visitors associate coastal North Carolina with summer vacations and warm weather. The presence of a strong quilting tradition might come as a surprise, but the temperature does drop, and winters get cold enough to make a quilt necessary for a good night's sleep.

In recent years a renewed interest in quilts has created a revival in this textile art. Community colleges and even public television offer quilting classes. Craft stores across the country market instruction manuals, books of quilt patterns, and quilting seminars. Classes and publications emphasize the artistic aspect of quilting.

Talking with some of this region's traditional quilters brings a more complete understanding of this craft. For these women, quilting provides a warm covering and the chance to demonstrate sewing skills. It also knits together the social fabric of the community.

Thelma Armstrong Mooney lives in the Pleasant Grove community on the eastern shore of Lake Mattamuskeet. Born in 1921, she learned quilting from her mother and her mother-in-law.

> We always quilted. I mean, this community always done their own quilting. My mother quilted, my mother-in-law quilted—all the community [quilted]. You made your quilt tops and then your bottoms. A lot of them was made out of feed bags. You'd put it together, and then you'd say [to your neighbor], 'Come and help me quilt.' When they had one you'd go there. Most times it was winter evenings. They didn't do it in the summertime because everyone was busy in the fields. When summertime come you didn't have time for that. It was just in the fall and winter when you couldn't do nothing else.

Good conversation turned the work of quilting into an entertaining and informative visit.

> Oh, you know how it is, we'd talk—talk, talk, talk! First one thing, then another; like who was sick and all that. They'd tell tales.
>
> The news, we'd get the news. That's the onliest news we had, 'cause we didn't have radios or TVs. After awhile we had a radio, but if we had company we didn't run [the radio].

Etta Mae Cuthrell of Killkenny enjoyed the social aspect of quilting even more.

My mama used to quilt with neighbors. They'd get her to come up and quilt with them…She quilted all over the neighborhood.

She'd do her work and fix her dinner, and then she'd cook enough for the last meal of the day. Then she'd go over to wherever she went [to quilt]. Most times she'd walk and she'd stay right there and quilt 'till ten or eleven o'clock. Just so she had a dip of snuff and them needles—that's all she cared about.

And she was a good quilter; her stitches were real teeny, and short. She really could quilt. I love to quilt as much as she did. I don't knot as good as she did, but almost as good.

Cuthrell recognizes the activity of quilting is good for her emotional health, and that it keeps her active mentally and socially.

I enjoy it…It keeps you busy. When you [quilt] you can sit down and think. We got a niece who lives in Gum Neck, and if she's got a vacant day, all I have to do is call her and she'll stay right here [and quilt]. She loves to quilt, too!

Virginia Pugh recalls quilting with great affection. Born in 1920 about a mile outside of Hyde County's Nebraska community, she recollects the names of three of her favorite quilt patterns: the "Cotton Leaf," "Church House Steps," and "Ring Around the Mountain."

The daughter of a freight boat captain, she had more free time for "quilting parties" than did the neighboring farm women.

People arrived [to quilt] around nine or ten o'clock in the morning and stayed until around three. You had to stew a pot of chicken to feed everybody. It was usually around eight people because you couldn't get more than two people on each side of the quilt. A quilt could be completed in one day, if people worked at it.

The women would talk and gossip while they quilted. Gossiping is when you're tending to someone else's business—keeping up with your neighbor.

Though the infirmities of age have slowed some of these women, those who can still quilt do so with enthusiasm. Those who cannot speak fondly of the important role quilting played in their lives. The same stitches that connect a quilt and form friends and neighbors into communities also bond generations to make a family. These women all learned the art of quilting from their families and passed their skill on to the next generation.

They beam with pride when reporting that their daughters, granddaughters, and nieces are continuing the tradition.

Perhaps quilting endures in this part of eastern North Carolina because it embodies the strength and comfort rural people find in their community. Making quilts unites small scraps of cloth into a larger whole. By themselves the scraps are useless. When joined together as a quilt, they make a covering that warms the body and pleases the eye. The process of assembling individual bits of cloth together brings neighbors and family together into a community which—like the quilt—provides comfort.

Quilting is a collective effort. Voluntary associations harness this collective energy in service to the larger community. Etta Mae Cuthrell, Thelma Mooney, and Virginia Pugh all report that local organizations use homemade quilts to raise money for charity. Pugh's church in the Nebraska community raffles a quilt; so does the Ladies' Aide Society at Mooney's church. Every Thanksgiving the Fairfield Volunteer Fire Department close to Cuthrell's home in Killkenny has a quilt raffle. The money raised by the sale of raffle tickets provides aid for the larger community.

Belief and Change

Hyde County hunters pose after a successful hunt, circa 1940: (left to right) Roy Mayo, Lathom Gibbs, Troy Mayo, Walt Williams and Biney Hodges.

Insiders and Outsiders

Trapping, hunting, and guiding hunters generate a great deal of folklore. The wildlife of Hyde County meets many local needs, and attracts the attention of outsiders. The natives profit from the outsiders who create jobs, bring novelty into an otherwise isolated region, and reinforce the community's identity. Their attention also has its drawbacks. People from outside the region contest the natives' understanding and use of resources. With an identity based on a tradition of hunting that stretches back for generations, the challenge from outsiders threatens the natives' self-concept—and, ultimately, their way of life. The tensions created by contact and conflict with these outsiders are apparent in the stories residents tell.

Conflict and Change

One matter of intense interest to the natives of this region is the arrival of corporate farms. These farms took control of the land from local farmers, and assigned farm management to people from outside the region. Not familiar with the customary role that trappers played, these outsiders challenged Marco Gibbs' ability to earn an income from trapping the land.

> When I was growing up…all the landowners wanted trapping done [on their property]. They [knew] how much damage could be done by 'coons and foxes in the chicken house. [Musk]rats in the field can damage ditches and cause canal banks to cave in.
>
> [Y]our corporate farms hired managers that weren't from here and didn't know about the damage that these animals could cause—and could care less. All they were interested in was making the money. To them, it looked like having a person trapping on their property could be more troublesome than the pests.
>
> It didn't take long [for them to find out]. The nutria really opened their eyes. I've seen tractors turned over and combines in the canals, from nutria and muskrats undermining their canal banks. I've seen trucks laying on their axle from where the animals' burrows caused the road to collapse.

Gibbs' experience with local conditions clearly demonstrated the importance of trapping traditions to corporate farmers. Some are now permitting him to trap on their lands.

The actions of outsiders confront the region's way of life in both overt and subtle ways. No challenges are more overt than the regulations imposed by government agencies. The presence of the Swan Quarter and Lake Mattamuskeet National Wildlife refuges in Hyde County joins the aggravation of federal wildlife regulations with state laws. Area residents address this conflict and deal with the tension through stories. The common theme of their stories is right versus might. Local citizens battle the perceived abuse of power perpetrated by unscrupulous government agents. Although the natives rarely win, the fact that they continue the struggle constitutes a moral victory.

A story from Maxine Simmons underscores the noxious reputation of game wardens.

> The game wardens were so exacting, and somewhat sneaky about what they did. If you angered one, then they sat on you. They'd watch you until you did something [wrong] and then sneak up on you.

[We] had a deep freezer. Well, friends would come down hunting and put a goose or a duck in there. We also had some quail in there, and [the game warden] knew about it.

At that time you were to keep federal game — the quail, the ducks, and the geese — until the fifteenth of February. You were supposed to be rid of it by then.

Well, it was in the freezer and they knew it. They were out to our house that night at 12:01 on February sixteenth — the head game warden, the sheriff, and the highway patrol. You'd have thought it was a criminal affair. They took food and carried it to Swan Quarter. They gave it to people over there instead of carrying it to social services where it was supposed to go. They gave it to people over there! We had several people call us and thank us for the game.

You talk about making somebody mad! I was furious! I was tempted, more times than one, to get the rifle and shoot. But I didn't.

Retired hunting guide Troy Mayo holds strong opinions about the limits of government. His stories of government excess help him fight back against abuse of power. Once he shot a duck and crippled the bird, but he didn't kill it. It fell inside the Mattamuskeet refuge's boundary.

The law says to get the crippled duck. It doesn't say anything about if it falls on the refuge or not. It says you are to make every reasonable effort to shoot a crippled duck.

I set my gun down outside the refuge and went inside its boundary with my dog. The duck was too alive to be taken with the dog, so I went and got my gun and shot it.

A federal warden was lying in the bushes watching to see if I'd break any more laws. When we come out of the woods he walked up and said, 'I saw you shoot that duck.' I asked where he was, and he told me he was hiding in the bushes. I couldn't believe he was hiding. I said, 'You could have been shot accidentally, and I'd be tried for murder.' [They charged me] with encroachment on the refuge with a firearm. Well, the warrant made no mention of a crippled duck. [The game warden] knew I was in the right to shoot it.

I asked the game warden what would have happened if I had not gone after the duck. He said he would have written me a ticket. In other words, I was going to get a ticket no matter what I did.

Another of Mayo's stories unmasks the perceived corrupt nature of the men assigned to enforce the law.

I took three fellows [hunting] one time. We had just got squared away in the blind when one of them said, 'We're all three state [game] wardens.' I said, 'Well, we'll hew to the line today.' They

SCOTT TAYLOR

Corporate farms took control of the land from local farmers and assigned farm management to people from outside of the region.

said, 'Oh, no! You treat us just like you do anybody else.' I said to myself, 'Yeah, we're going to hew to the line.'

Anyway, game wasn't moving too swift, and I took my dog and got out on the bank. I looked, and coming across the lake there was six or seven geese coming right there to the blind. Them geese got in and sat down outside the decoys—just out of range.

I heard them shucking shells out of their guns. All of a sudden, they opened up on those geese on the water and just rolled them over! They [wardens] were laughing and carrying on. My dog went out there and retrieved the geese.

I got back in the blind and they asked me, 'Do you know what we shot those birds with?' I said, 'Don't tell me nothing!' I knew they shot them with buckshot, which was illegal.

BILL MANSFIELD

Their use of outlawed ammunition places them above the law. The unsportsmanlike tactic of shooting birds on the water places them beyond contempt.

These stories of the agents' abuse of power are quite common. Only rarely does one hear tales that boast the local hunters' triumph over the power of the state. People still talk about the time Rufus Carawan was tried for poaching and talked his way out of court. He did not deny the charges, but spoke with conviction about the need to provide for his family. Carawan's eloquence moved the judge to tears and won his release.

In another story, a Hyde County hunter recognizes a federal game warden in a local store and puts one over on him. To irritate the game warden, he begins boasting about the large amount of game he has poached. Provoked, the game warden approaches the hunter: "Sir, do you know who I am? I'm the federal game warden for Atlanta." Unimpressed, the hunter

The hunting lodge at Lake Mattamuskeet has hosted hunters from across the country and around the world.

counters: "Do you know who I am? I'm the biggest liar in Hyde County."

In the first story, Carawan uses the truth to overcome an injustice imposed by the law. By sharing the story, hunters share in Carawan's victory. In the second story the anonymous hunter uses humor to mock and deflate the game warden's power. Recounting that story allows local hunters to "tweak the nose" of authority. The stories surrounding encounters between wildlife officials and local hunters demonstrate the adversarial nature of this relationship. They are one of the few forms of resistance open to the people of Hyde County.

Stories generated around the relationship between visiting hunters and natives reflect a more complex association. The sportsmen's presence boosts the region's economy. "Hunting," as Seth Bridgeman Credle put it, "has brought many a dollar into Hyde County." Troy Mayo's comment echoes his friend. "Oh, yeah, that's the livelihood of this area. You do away with [hunting] and this country'd be in a predicament."

For years, sportsmen vacationing in Hyde County have provided relief from the daily routine, and placed an otherwise-isolated community in contact with a larger society. Seth Bridgeman Credle recalls his days as a hunting guide as "…a lot of fun. You'd meet some good fine people. It was a pleasure to see them shoot."

As soon as she was old enough, Betty Mann helped her mother board the hunters that her father, Joe Simmons, guided.

> We couldn't wait for hunting season to start. There were so many people and that was the only time you saw them. You always had your favorites in every group. I liked the ones that laughed and talked with me.
>
> My sister married a boy that [came] down here hunting with his father for years. Well, even before then it was just like family.

Martin Armstrong remembers some of the fringe benefits of guiding wealthy hunters.

> In them days they'd tip you well and you'd get a lot of money out of them. If they had some liquor when they left, they'd leave that with you. They'd leave their shotgun shells, too. I ended every season with a case of shells.

Armstrong also received invitations to join wealthy hunters at their clubs in Maryland and New York. Troy Mayo accepted an invitation to accompany a hunting trip to Canada, and obtained a fine shotgun as a gift from a wealthy hunter. Edward "Bunk" Carawan tells a similar story.

> My father used to guide this man from Argentina. He was a millionaire. When he'd come down

he'd drive a Lincoln automobile. He'd pass the keys to my father and say, 'While I'm here, take your family anywhere you want to. Here're the keys to my car.' Dad liked to see the man come 'cause he paid him a hundred dollars a day. Man, that was money!

George and Geraldine Bush truly profited from their contacts with hunters. They housed and guided an executive from the Newport News shipyard. This contact helped their son win a place in the shipyard's apprentice training program, and their daughter a job in the shipyard's office.

Sportsmen made Hyde County a vacation destination, thus validating the region and its culture. Visitors' enjoyment of the everyday fare gave residents a new appreciation of their diet. Maxine Simmons recalls visiting hunters being more concerned with eating than hunting. "They said, 'We don't care [about hunting], what we want is food.' They kept me busy in the kitchen. One man talked so much about Hyde County cooking, his wife came down here to check it out."

Yet, even as visiting hunters confirm Hyde County's culture, they also undermine it. Simply by their presence, visitors offer an alternative to the natives' way of life. Affluent visitors might present a greater threat because of their material wealth and access to resources. Some of the visiting hunters upset the status quo by challenging the guides' expertise as hunters. Occasionally—through ignorance or carelessness—the visitors threaten a guide's life.

The hunting guides confront the tension of such situations through the stories they tell about the hunters they guide. While they describe the fringe benefits of guiding wealthy hunters, most of their stories present people of modest means as the preferred parties to guide. Wealthy people are portrayed as difficult and stingy. Seth Bridgeman Credle most enjoyed guiding "somebody who works for a living." His friend Troy Mayo concurs. "Factory workers are the best tippers," he claims. "Doctors and lawyers the worst." Edward "Bunk" Carawan sums up the problem of guiding wealthy hunters.

These guys that had plenty of money always thought they could buy everything that they wanted. And they would complain. They'd say things like, 'Why isn't the birds here? Why didn't they come this way? Why did they go that way?'

Seth Bridgeman Credle tells a similar story.

Once in a while a doctor will tell you how much money you're making [guiding him]. You furnished the boat, the decoys, the blind, and you were getting eighteen dollars. If you spent more than fifteen minutes with the doctor, he'd a gotten more money from you than that. The whole time he's telling you, 'Boy, you got it made, you're getting rich.'

Once a man fell out with me because nothing flew all day. He was griping to me about it. He acted like it was my fault that nothing wasn't flying. But I ain't got nothing to do with it.

Edward "Bunk" Carawan's story illustrates how he manages the threat posed by wealthy hunters.

One of the days I enjoyed the most is when I carried this old man from Richmond, Virginia. That man could see stuff. It was a little before [sunrise], and the sky was red. He said, 'My Lord! This is paradise! That's the most beautiful sight I've ever seen!'

All day long that man said, 'This is paradise, this is paradise.' Well, we stayed there all day. He was enjoying it so much I just enjoyed watching him.

He said, 'I've sat in my office, pulled on my cigar and worried about a telephone call and another dollar. I never knew what nature provided. I didn't know the beauty of this world. I'll be back.'

The story validates Carawan's heritage. Despite the hunter's elite status in Richmond, he envied Carawan. Hyde County's rural setting and way of life were elevated over his affluent urban existence.

Visiting hunters who presume to know more about the wildlife and the territory than the guides they hire are a source of frustration. The guides handle this irritation by characterizing hunters as inept in their stories. Seth Bridgeman Credle talks about the problems of guiding inexperienced hunters.

Used to be Christmas and Thanksgiving was a time for boys to hunt in the lake. Folks would bring their boys to hunt.

All of them were not as bad as some, but some were just as wild as rats in the blind. The boys would be jumping up and down, breaking the bushes, and looking up to see what was coming. They would scare the game away. Their old man would wonder why didn't the game come? He should be able to see that his sons are scaring the game away.

Inexperienced hunters frighten away game, but also frighten the guides. The dangers of using high-powered firearms in close proximity to others are apparent. Martin Armstrong recalled an incident when he was serving as a guide for some children.

None of them were over seventeen. We got in the blind and one of those boy's guns went off. It didn't hurt nobody. I told them, 'Boys, you're going to have to do different from this or we can't hunt.

Now sit your guns down [and] don't mess with them until I tell you to.'

They caught on damn quick. They were all right from then on. You must be particular about stuff like that.

Troy Mayo tells a similar story about guiding a doctor and his son.

I kept telling that doctor's son about gun safety. I said, 'Look, that gun can go off!' Well, he set it off! He turned white as a sheet—scared the daylights out of him.

It made me hot! What I told that dude! I made that boy promise me he'd never point a gun at nobody! It made a believer out of him. He was a little smarty dude.

That's what you had to be wary about in guiding, somebody shooting you. That was your first thought when you had a party of hunters. It stayed on my mind until they showed me they were safe hunters.

Edward "Bunk" Carawan describes a trigger-happy deer hunter.

My father had a party of patrolmen one time. He put the dogs out and I was with them. All at once we hear the dogs running and coming up through the reeds. The patrolman threwed his gun up [to shoot].

I yelled, 'Hold it! Put that gun down! Don't you shoot until that deer gets out here and you can see what you're shooting at.' Well, that 'deer' popped out [of the reeds] and it was my father!

Some of these guys just shoot by sound. A lot of people get killed. It's foolish for a man to get shot. With as many hunters out shooting with high-powered guns it's lucky more people aren't killed. I don't never shoot until I know what I'm shooting *at*.

Joe Simmons was not so lucky. A careless accident from an inexperienced hunter cost him his leg, and nearly took his life. His wife tells the story, portraying the men responsible for injuring her husband as inept and unscrupulous.

A man from Winston-Salem shot Joe accidentally—carelessly. They were checking their guns to see that the safety was on. The man had a new double-barreled shotgun, and he hit Joe below the knee with both barrels.

He cried out, 'You've shot me!' That didn't register with them, so he cried out again, 'You've shot me!'

He said those men went absolutely all to pieces. They got down on the ground like animals. He had a time getting them straightened up.

Joe Simmons directed his own rescue. He instructed the hunters to remove their boot laces for tourniquets, told them how to make a stretcher from their coats, and figured out the best route to get the car to the blind. The man who shot Simmons paid the hospital bill, but—fearing a lawsuit—he placed all of his property in his father's name. Adding insult to injury, the hunter never visited the guide he shot.

Casting the visiting hunters as miscreants, Simmons' wife places them outside the community of knowledgeable and trustworthy Hyde County hunters. She also reaffirms the values of her culture.

COURTESY MAXINE SIMMONS

A careless accident from an inexperienced hunter cost Joe Simmons his leg and nearly took his life.

SCOTT TAYLOR

A family graveyard overlooks a newly plowed field on a Hyde County farm.

Witch Hunts

The narratives collected about trapping and hunting represent the current system of beliefs, reinforce the collective identity, and help people reconcile the divisions in their culture. However, a small number of the stories appear to represent a belief system no longer current in the region—or at least one not usually discussed with strangers. This belief system uses supernatural events to explain the bewildering animal world and to span the gulf separating the souls of animals from the souls of humans. Three senior citizens from this region told basically the same story to explain elusive game. In these stories, a supernatural being—neither human nor animal—assumes an animal's form and leads hunters on a difficult, and ultimately frustrating, chase.

As a child, Thelma Mooney heard a story of hunters frustrated in pursuit of squirrels. As they passed a woman's house the woman cried out, "Boys, you needn't go a-squirreling. You won't kill nary a one." The hunters saw one squirrel, but they couldn't seem to kill it. "They'd shoot it off the limb and it'd get back on. They messed with that squirrel all day long and didn't hit it once." Transformed into the shape of a squirrel, the woman focused the hunter's attention on an "animal" they could not have, thwarting the hunt.

In a conversation about supernatural occurrences, one elderly man mentioned an unusually large white rabbit "as big as a dog" that could not be shot. He then proceeded to tell a story very similar to Mooney's. In his story, the witch is a man who takes the shape of a deer. The frustrated hunters replace the lead shot in their guns with silver coins. They wound the elusive "deer" with the silver bullet, and the wounded deer leads then to the man's home. There the hunters discover the man wounded just like the deer.

David Hopkins, a retired waterman from eastern Beaufort County, tells a more detailed version of the story.

There used to be an old lady that lived up there by the name of Miss Ridder. That was before I come in the world. Old Miss Ridder was a witch, now that's a fact!

There was a lot of the men that deer hunted. [In] them days they hunted on horseback. She would tell them where to go to jump a buck. She'd tell them, 'You go right there and you'll jump him. You'll jump a nice buck—one of the nicest you've ever seen.'

Well, they listened at her. They'd jump the buck, but didn't never get him. The buck would get away. A time or two before that, their dogs would be a-running [a deer] and old Miss Ridder would appear out on the sand hill with her apron full of lightered knots. I've heared one of the men that hunted tell that.

Eventually they found out what was going on. She was a witch and they didn't know it. They

SCOTT TAYLOR

Thelma Mooney is a generous hostess with a wealth of traditional knowledge, including planting by the signs, home cooking, quilting techniques, and ghost stories.

cut silver [coins] and put in their guns, and they went out and shot her.

The dogs run [a deer]. They shot her [in the form of a deer] and ruined one of her legs. That silver went in her leg. This is a fact to my own knowing.

These stories attempt to explain the unexplainable and represent an older belief system. One clue of their age is the fact that they are in no way connected with commercial hunting. This indicates that the stories developed before hunting became a money-making endeavor.

Stories about hunters, wardens, and witches offer insight to a portion of the collective knowledge—the folk culture—of this place. Though told by individuals about separate occurrences, their common themes suggest a shared belief system. Shared belief systems are a result of the collective experiences of people engaged in similar activities in the same environment.

The stories instruct both the tellers and their audience in understanding animal behavior and human nature. They also act as cautionary tales, reminding the community to be wary of game wardens and unfamiliar hunters. The stories reinforce the community's identity, upholding commonly held values and setting the natives apart from outsiders.

Conclusion

My official research has ended, but I continue to visit the region. Although deadlines and budget limited the scope of this project, I gained a greater understanding of, and affection for, eastern North Carolina. I developed an appreciation of the landscape's subtle beauty, and the open-hearted people who live there.

Thinking about the stories told to me by coastal Carolinians has helped me reach a new understanding of folklore and the process of tradition. In an effort to fully understand folklore's complexities, scholars too often separate the folk from the lore. This is akin to studying an animal isolated in a zoo; you learn a great deal about the individual animal, but very little about how the animal interacts with its natural environment. In a similar fashion, contemplating tradition disconnected from people diminishes its reality, and perpetuates the notion that folklore belongs to history. Observing traditions surrounded by the everyday circumstances that produce them demonstrates that folklore is an ongoing process and not a relic of the past. A couple of examples illustrate the point.

I observed a tradition at work one December afternoon as Ted Cahoon, his cousins, and his uncle Edison Cahoon skinned a deer. The deer's carcass hung from a dressing rack suspended on a pine tree in the backyard of Edison's house. Ted is a practiced hunter but lacks his uncle's deer-skinning experience. The older man supervised the younger hunter's work, guiding his actions with praise and, when necessary, ridicule. Much teasing followed a hasty error when the young hunter accidentally opened the deer's intestines, spilling partially digested food on the fresh meat. Edison, however, assured Ted that the deer meat was not spoiled and praised him for not rupturing other body parts such as the deer's full bladder, which would render the meat inedible. As they removed the deer's bladder, the conversation turned to alternative uses for various parts of the deer. The hunters told stories about using urine from the deer's bladder as an excellent lure for deer. Deer antlers supposedly command a good price because Asians grid them into powder and use them as aphrodisiacs. Though he is not sure why, Edison said that Asians pay fabulous amounts of money for a bear's gall bladder. This comment generated stories about bear hunts. Before long, some whiskey appeared and fueled a conversation that rambled from the talents of hunting dogs, to the qualities of country singers. Thus, a family passed on traditions. Through informal, "hands-on" instruction, a young man learns the fine art of eviscerating a deer. And perhaps more important, the "casual" conversation surrounding this process also instructs and reinforces the community belief system—offering lessons in "alternative medicine" and entrepreneurship, hunting techniques, dog training, and musical aesthetics. These stories provide the means of taking to heart and understanding the reality of their experience.

Research on Hyde County's community music offered another opportunity to see the transmission of traditions. My quest for community-based music led me to Charles Cahoon, who plays harmonica for a local ensemble known as "The Blue's Lords." This quartet of white Hyde County musicians originally formed in the mid-1970s inspired by the idea of playing electrified "Chicago Blues." For the most part, they performed for their own enjoyment at local parties, but occasionally they played an out-of-town engagement. Eventually, jobs and family obligations ended the band except for infrequent "reunion" parties.

The band's contact with a couple of local, older African-American blues musicians known to the white musicians only by their nicknames—"Doo Buddy" and "Bo Diddley"—intrigued me. I was disappointed to discover that they had passed on. Blues music from elderly black men is easily labeled traditional. Lacking the patina of age and validation of race, the Blues Lords' place in tradition is more complicated. However, their place is no less valuable. I realized this when I attended one of their reunion parties and left with a new understanding of the everyday nature of traditions.

The Blues Lords held their party in "downtown" Swan Quarter on a February night. The setting was pretty basic. Friends and families of the band had cleared out an old garage and set up some chairs and a couple of tables. Coffee brewed in an urn, while beer chilled in ice chests. The band's equipment occupied one corner of the room and a banner above the drum riser proclaimed: "THE PARTY IS HERE!" That night, their repertoire ranged from blues and blues-based soul to rock music, with a hearty dose of country tunes mixed in.

Although the use of electrically amplified instruments and their reliance on music from commercial sources obscured the Blues Lords' traditional form, a closer examination reveals the band's solid place in southern traditional and vernacular music. The distinctive sound of southern vernacular music is primarily the result of blending musical traditions from the British Isles and Africa. This euphonious hybrid of traditions first achieved national popularity in the mid-nineteenth century with music from minstrel shows. It resurfaced again in the middle of the twentieth century when rock-and-roll swept the world.

The Blues Lords pay homage to the British Isles ballad tradition with their narrative country and western songs, while their blues and blues-based material springs from ancient African roots. Using electrical instruments and relying on commercial music sources parallel the ways in which minstrel music influenced southern vernacular music. The use of these items represents a dynamic and long-standing relationship between commercial music and traditional music. The give and take between traditional and commercial music makes their performance acceptable to conservative listeners, yet innovative enough to new listeners.

While the form of the Blues Lords' music might not immediately be identified as traditional, its function clearly is. Just as the square dance music of the Barber Shanty string bands provided a focal point for the community, the music of the blues band brings neighbors together. Once assembled, they visit, court, dance, drink, and forget about the burdens of the day. Ostensibly, the community gathers for an evening of music and dance, but in the process they affirm the values they share. The young acquire musical preferences, cultivate dance styles, and learn social behavior modeled on the examples set by their elders.

Folklore and the ageless process of tradition continue amid the trappings of modernity. These are the lessons that the people of Hyde County taught me.

About the Author

Bill Mansfield grew up in Raleigh, NC. He graduated from St. Andrews College in Laurinburg in 1977 and received a master's degree in folklore from the University of North Carolina at Chapel Hill in 1992. His interest in folklife studies comes from listening to his mother and grandparents tell stories about rural life in Chatham County.

Mansfield has worked as a folklorist from one end of the state to the other. In 1982 he researched life on Portsmouth Island for Cape Lookout National Seashore, and in the mid-1990s he served as the staff folklorist at Western Carolina University's Mountain Heritage Center. Most recently, he has documented folklife in eastern North Carolina. Mansfield and his wife, Lu Ann Jones, call Greenville, NC home, but he is currently on assignment with the National Park Service in Atlanta, GA.

North Carolina's Northeast Partnership is dedicated to increasing the standard of living for citizens in its 16-county region through industrial and business development and tourism. The public and private partnership strives to improve economic conditions in Northeast North Carolina by marketing the region's excellent business, tourism, and quality-of-life amenities.

The 16 counties that comprise the regional partnership are: Beaufort, Bertie, Camden, Chowan, Currituck, Dare, Gates, Halifax, Hertford, Hyde, Martin, Northampton, Pasquotank, Perquimans, Tyrrell and Washington. For more information about North Carolina's Northeast Partnership, visit the partnership's website at www.ncnortheast.com.

The North Carolina Arts Council is a division of the North Carolina Department of Cultural Resources, the nation's first cabinet-level state agency for the arts, history, and libraries. An important part of the arts council's mission since its inception in 1967 has been to enrich the cultural life of the state.

The Folklife Program has been part of the North Carolina Arts Council for more than 20 years, supporting artists and projects that document and present North Carolina's rich traditional culture. It works to promote public knowledge and appreciation of the state's folk arts and folklife resources, and participates in a wide range of projects, including cultural tourism and arts in education. To learn more about folklife, the arts, and cultural tourism in North Carolina, visit www.ncarts.org.

Hyde County Attractions

"Take the road less traveled, to a place where time seems to move a little slower."

**Mattamuskeet National Wildlife Refuge
and Swan Quarter National Wildlife Refuge**
38 Mattamuskeet Refuge Rd., Swan Quarter, NC 27885
(252) 926-4021

*Alligator River National Wildlife Refuge
P.O. Box 1969, Manteo, NC 27954
(252) 473-1668

*Pocosin Lakes National Wildlife Refuge
3255 Shore Dr., Creswell, NC 27928
(252) 797-4431

*Gull Rock Gameland
(919) 733-7291

*Cape Hatteras National Seashore and Ocracoke Campground
Rt. 1 Box 675, Manteo, NC 27954
(252) 473-2111

**Mattamuskeet Lodge
On National Register of Historic Places.
38 Mattamuskeet Refuge Rd., Swan Quarter, NC 27885
(252) 926-9171

**Historic Ocracoke
Entire village on National Register of Historic Places and includes the 1823 Ocracoke Lighthouse and the British Cemetery.

Ocracoke Preservation Society and Museum
49 Water Plant Rd., Ocracoke, NC 27960
(252) 928-7375

Hyde County's Talking Houses & Historic Places Tour
A driving tour of ten historic sites on the mainland and Ocracoke Island. Each is equipped with an AM radio transmitter with 4.5 minutes of recorded historical information that can be tuned to from the convenience of your car.

Lake Mattamuskeet
North Carolina's largest natural lake with fishing, hunting, bird-watching, flora and fauna, and other wildlife.

Historic Lake Landing Landmarks
A driving tour of the Lake Landing National Register Historic District.

Ocracoke Island
Accessible only by boat, ferry or plane. A unique step back in time.

Pamlico Scenic Byway, Alligator River Route Scenic Byway, and Outer Banks Scenic Byway
Three of 44 N.C. Department of Transportation Scenic Byways traverse through Hyde County.

*Although these attractions are in Hyde County, their contact addresses are outside of the county.
**These attractions are part of the historic Albemarle Tour.

For more information on mainland and Ocracoke Island, NC, contact the Greater Hyde County Chamber of Commerce:

P. O. Box 178, Swan Quarter, NC 27885   toll free (888) 493-3826 or (252) 926-9171
www.albemarle-nc.com/hyde   www.ocracoke-nc.com   e-mail: hydecocc@beachlink.com